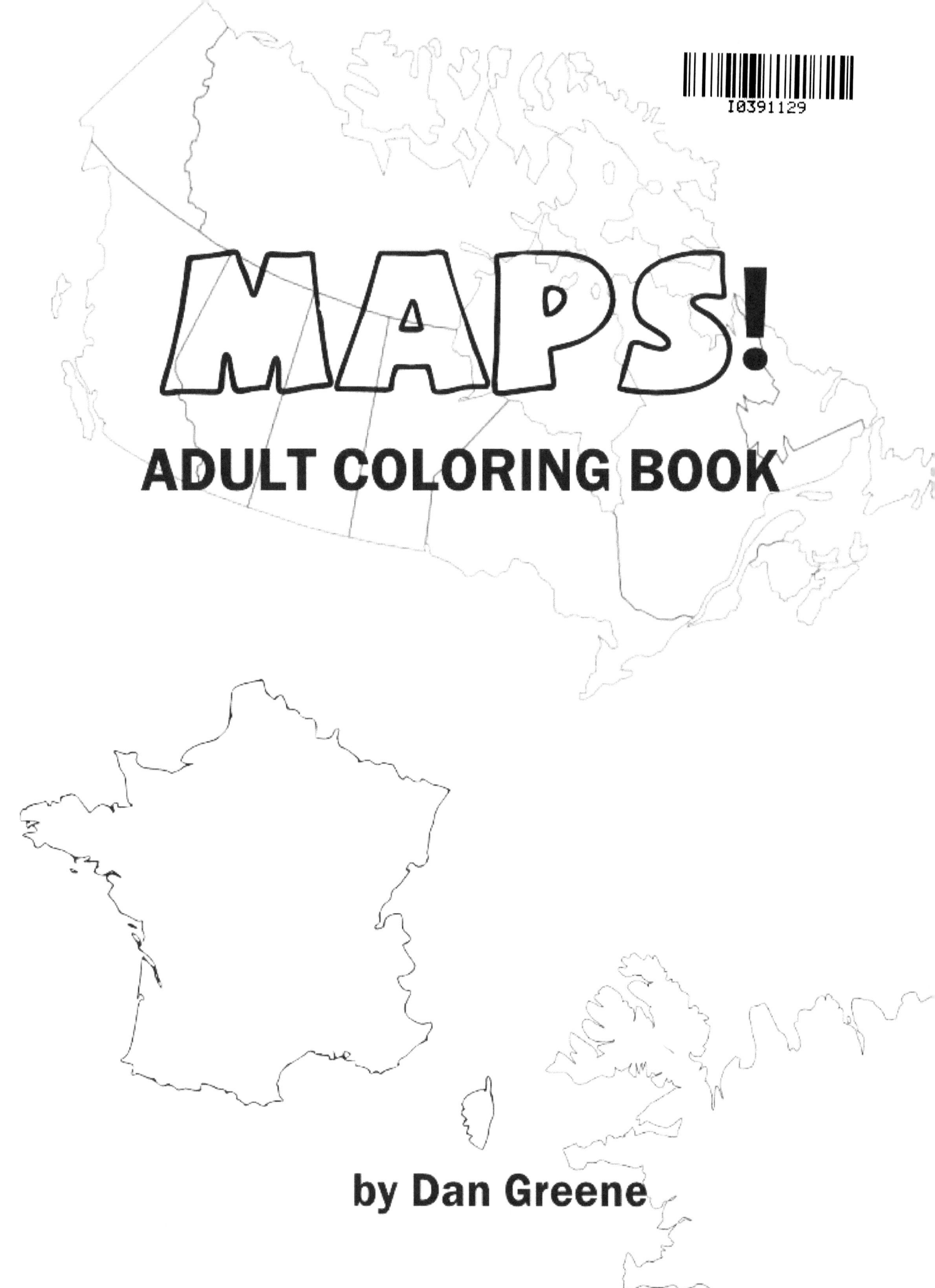

MAPS!

ADULT COLORING BOOK

by Dan Greene

DEDICATION

This book is dedicated to everyone whose favorite part of Social Studies was coloring in maps, and to my son Victor, with love beyond latitude & longitude.

HAVE FUN!

AFRICA

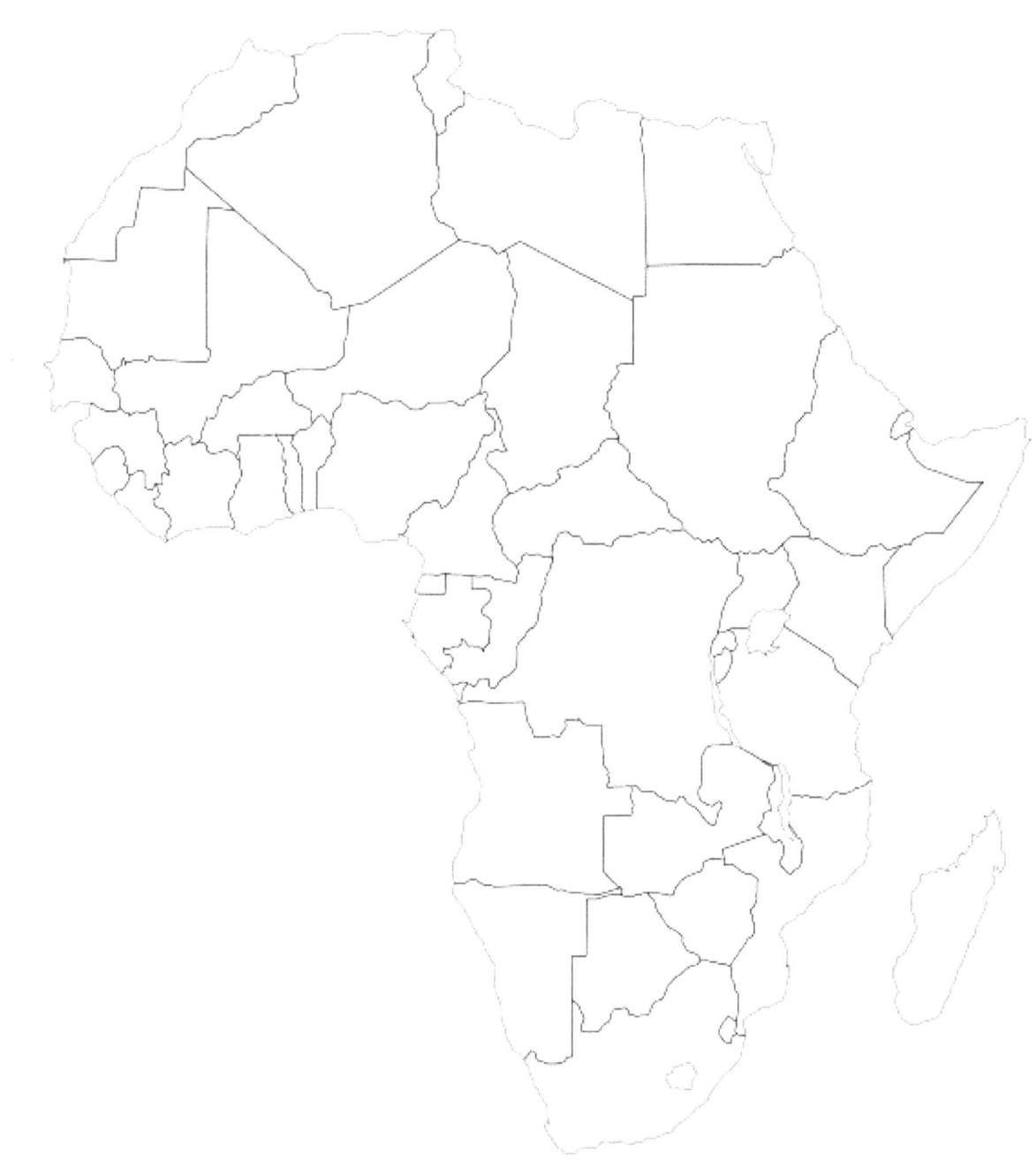

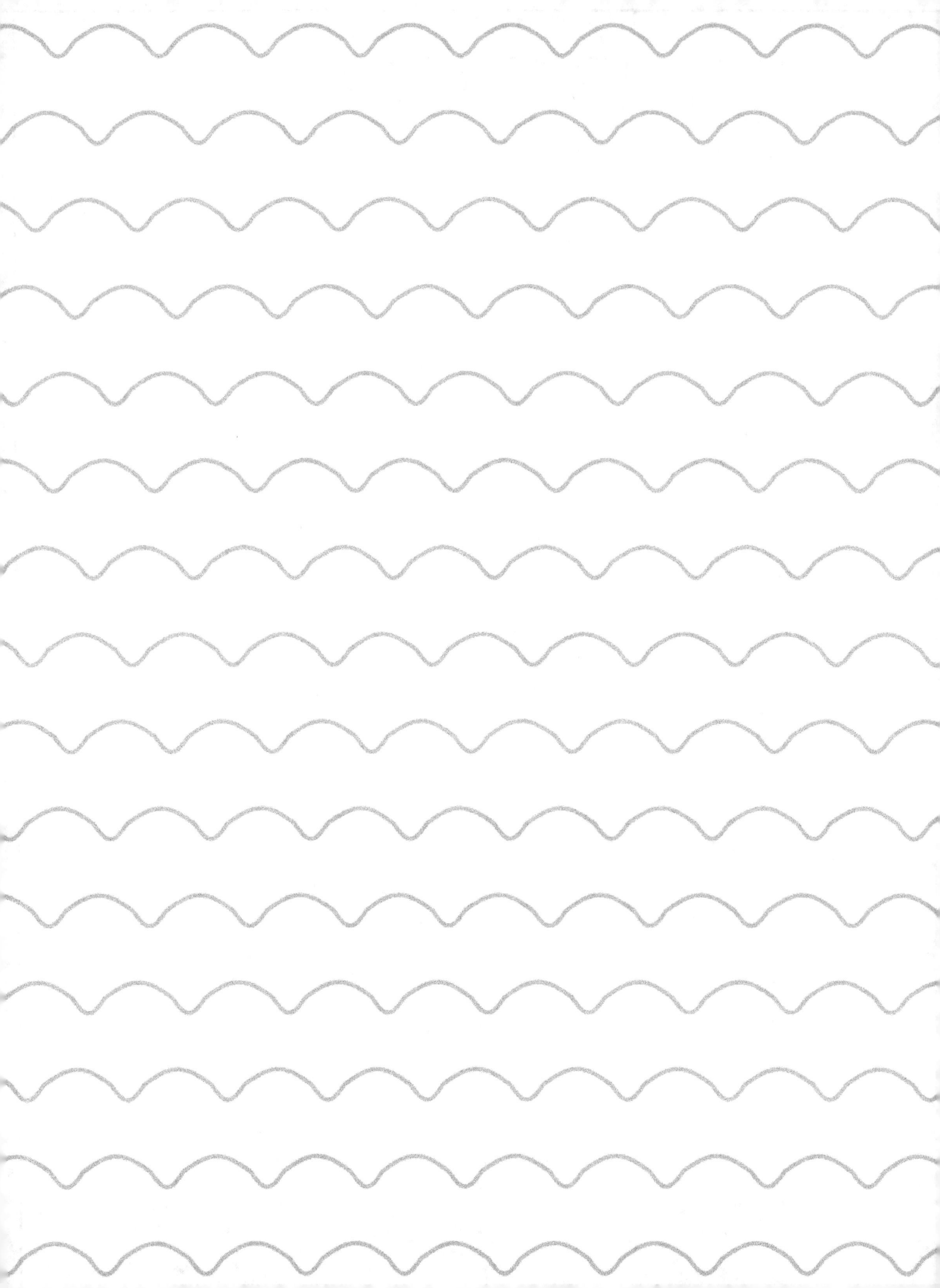

ANTARCTICA

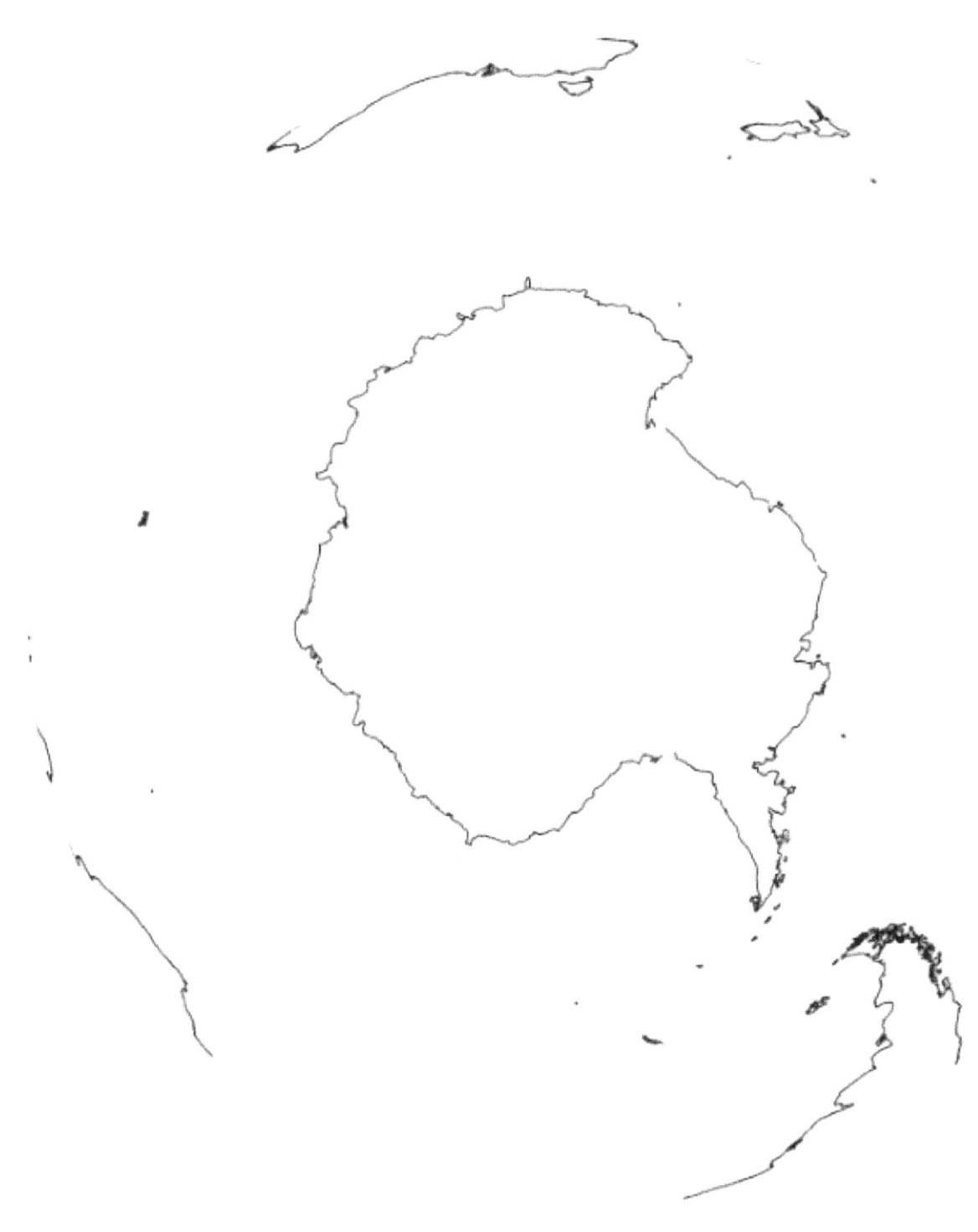

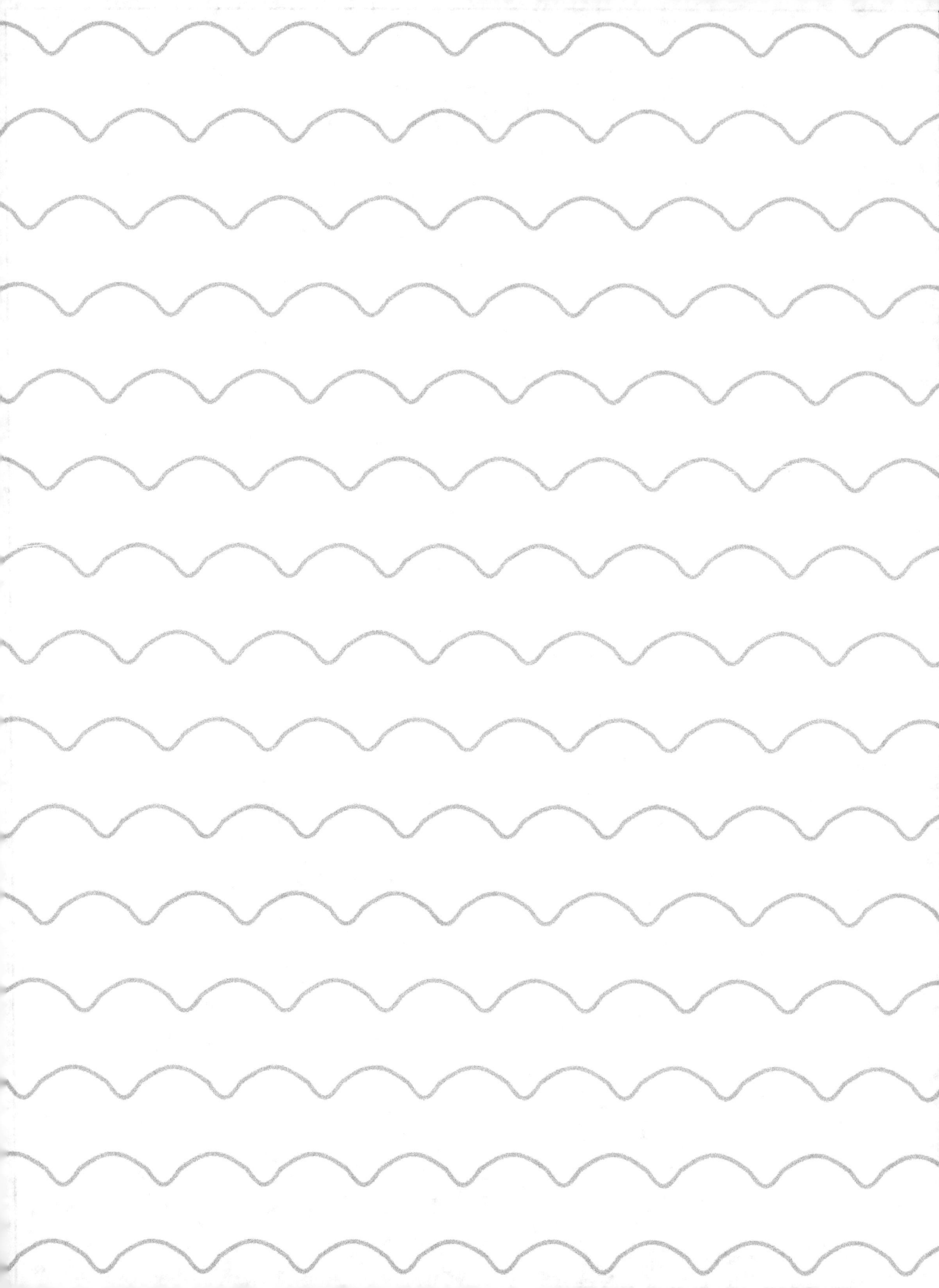

ASIA

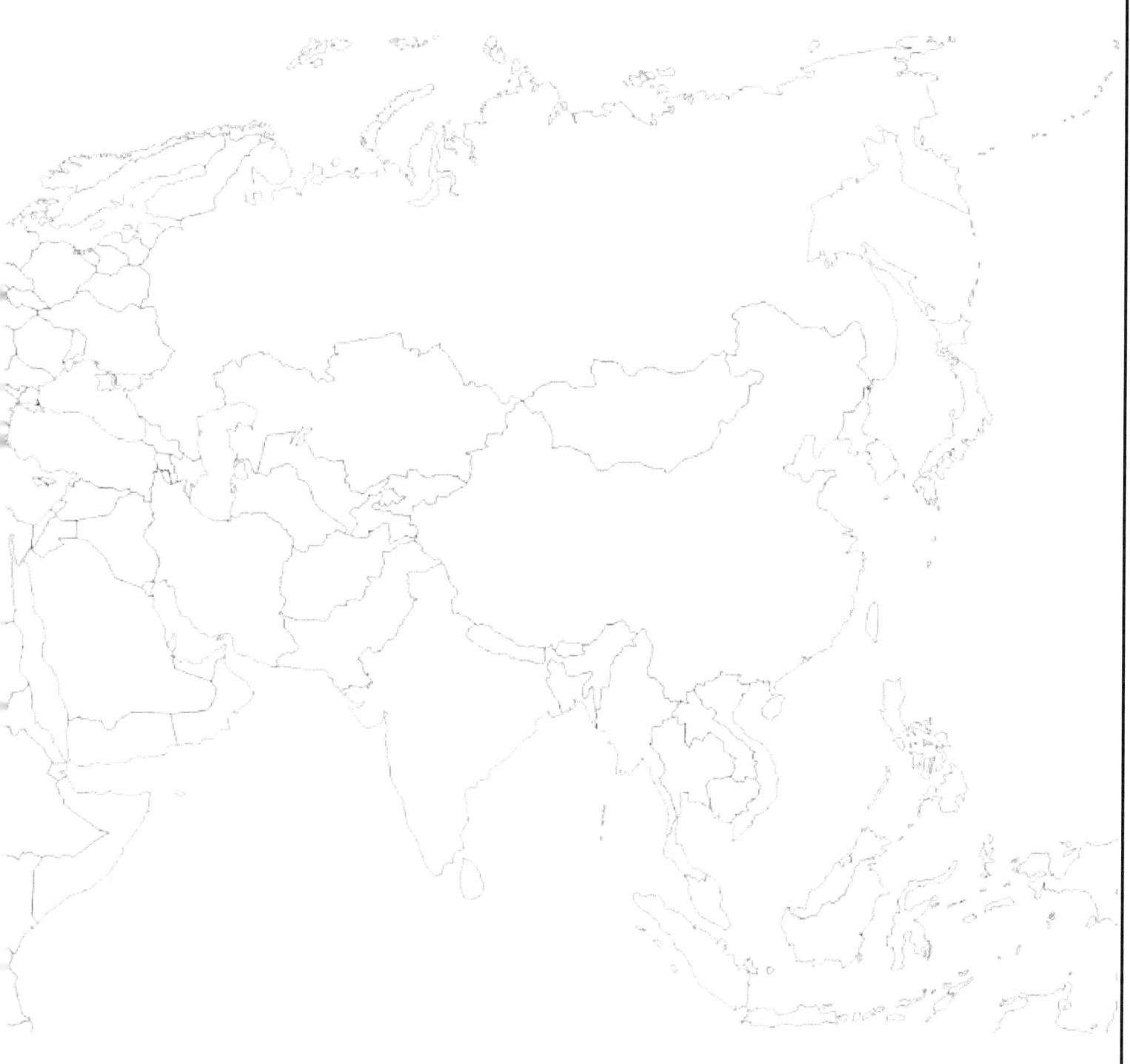

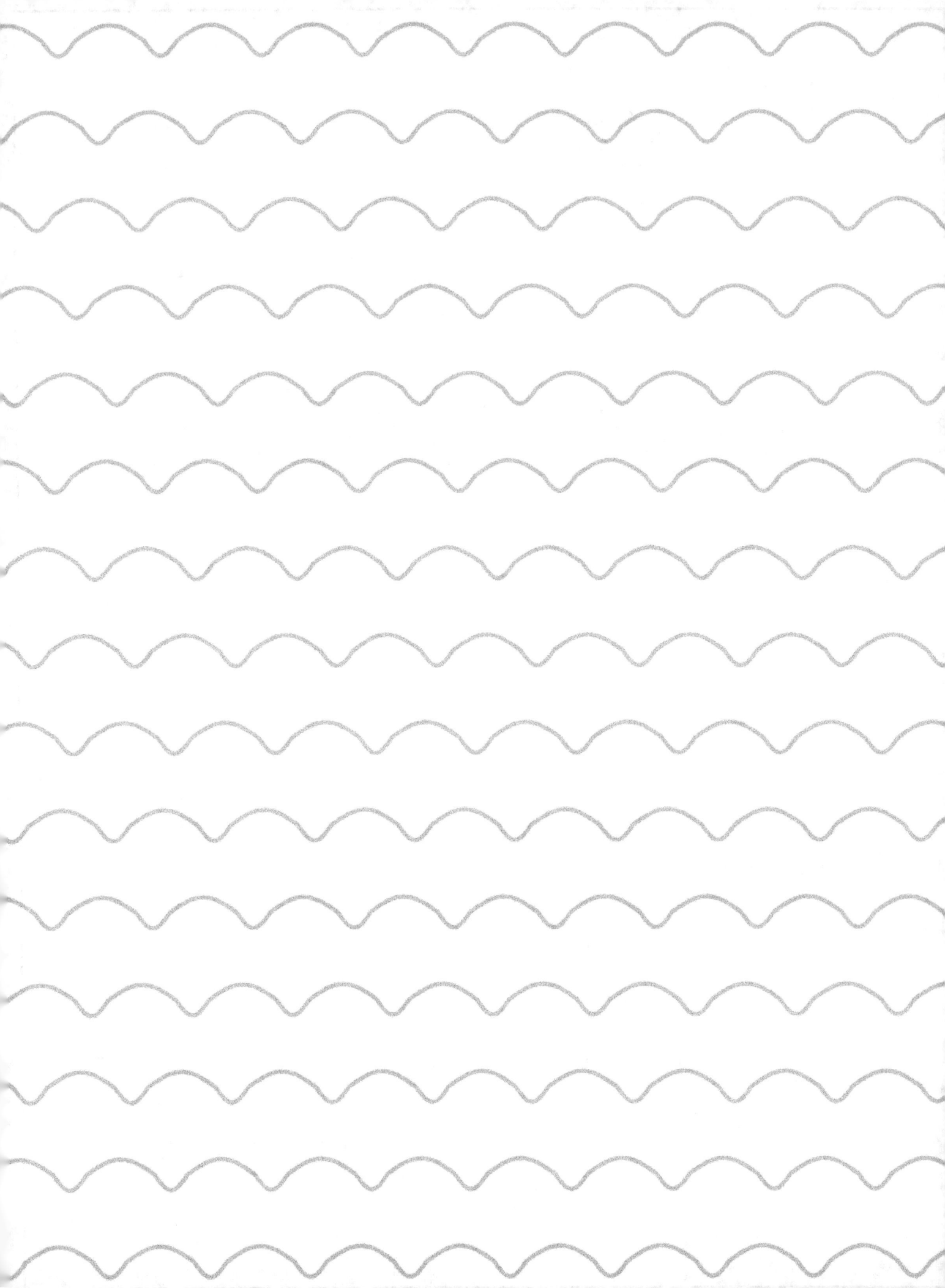

AUSTRALIA

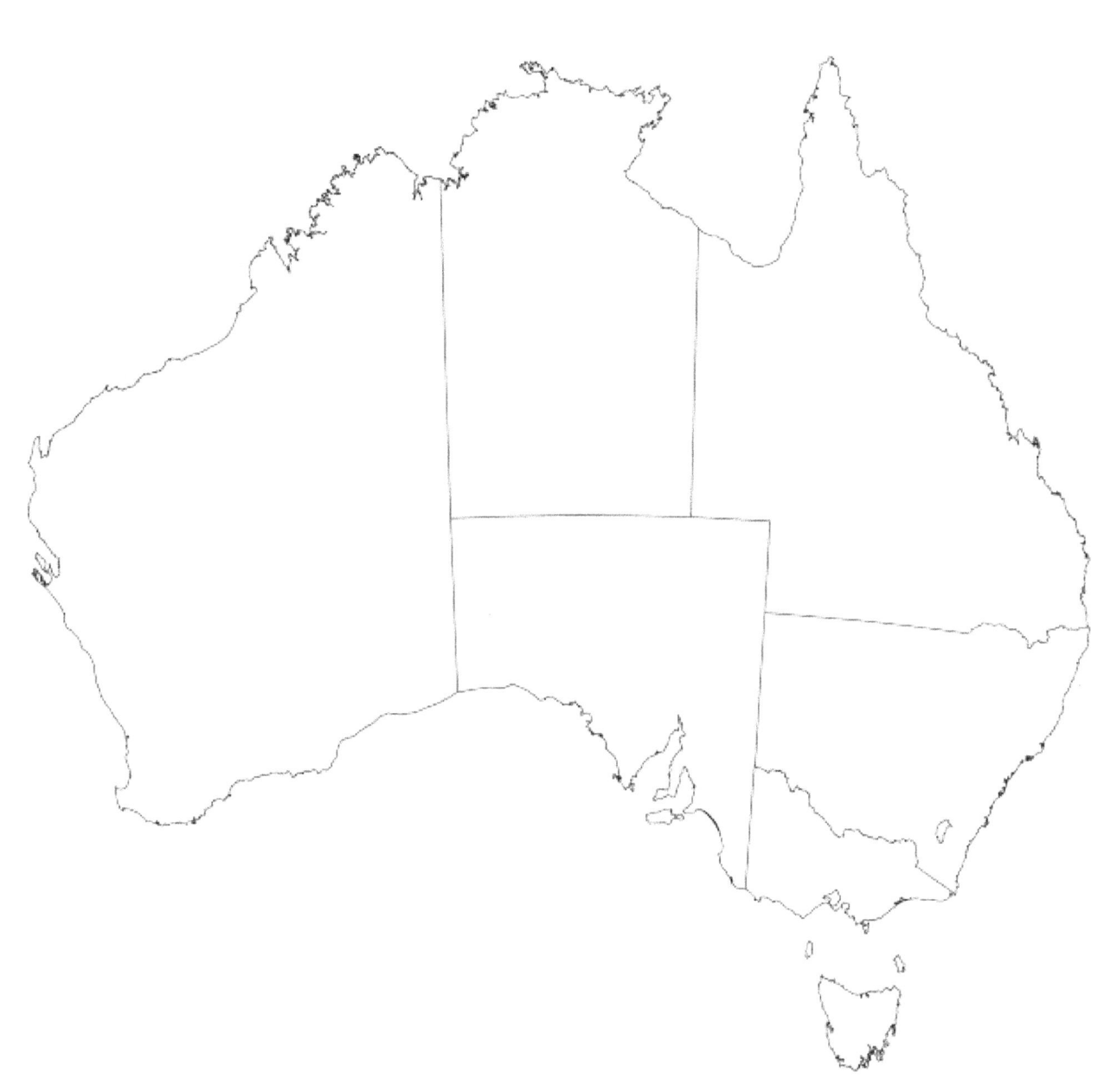

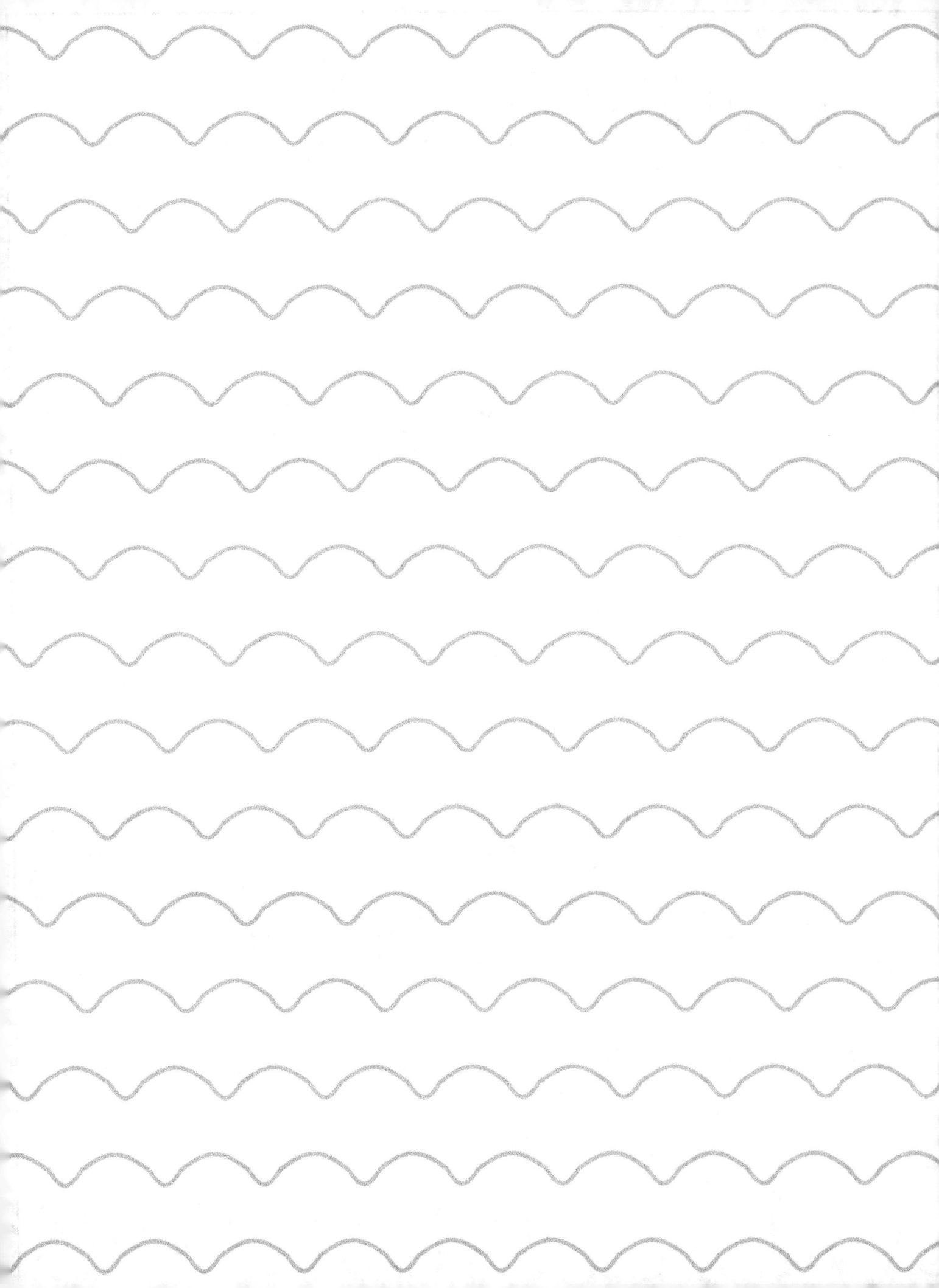

THE BRITISH

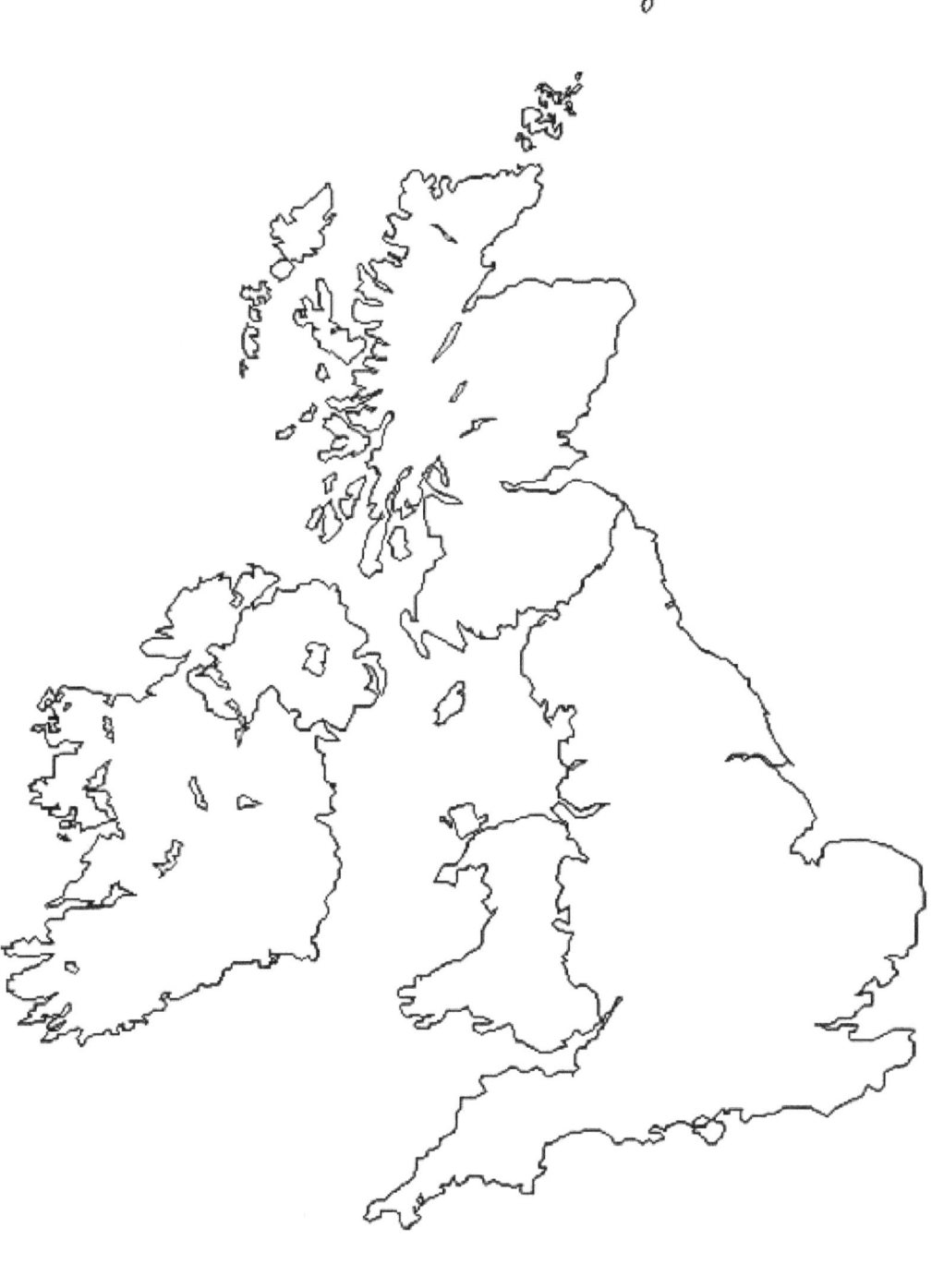

ISLES

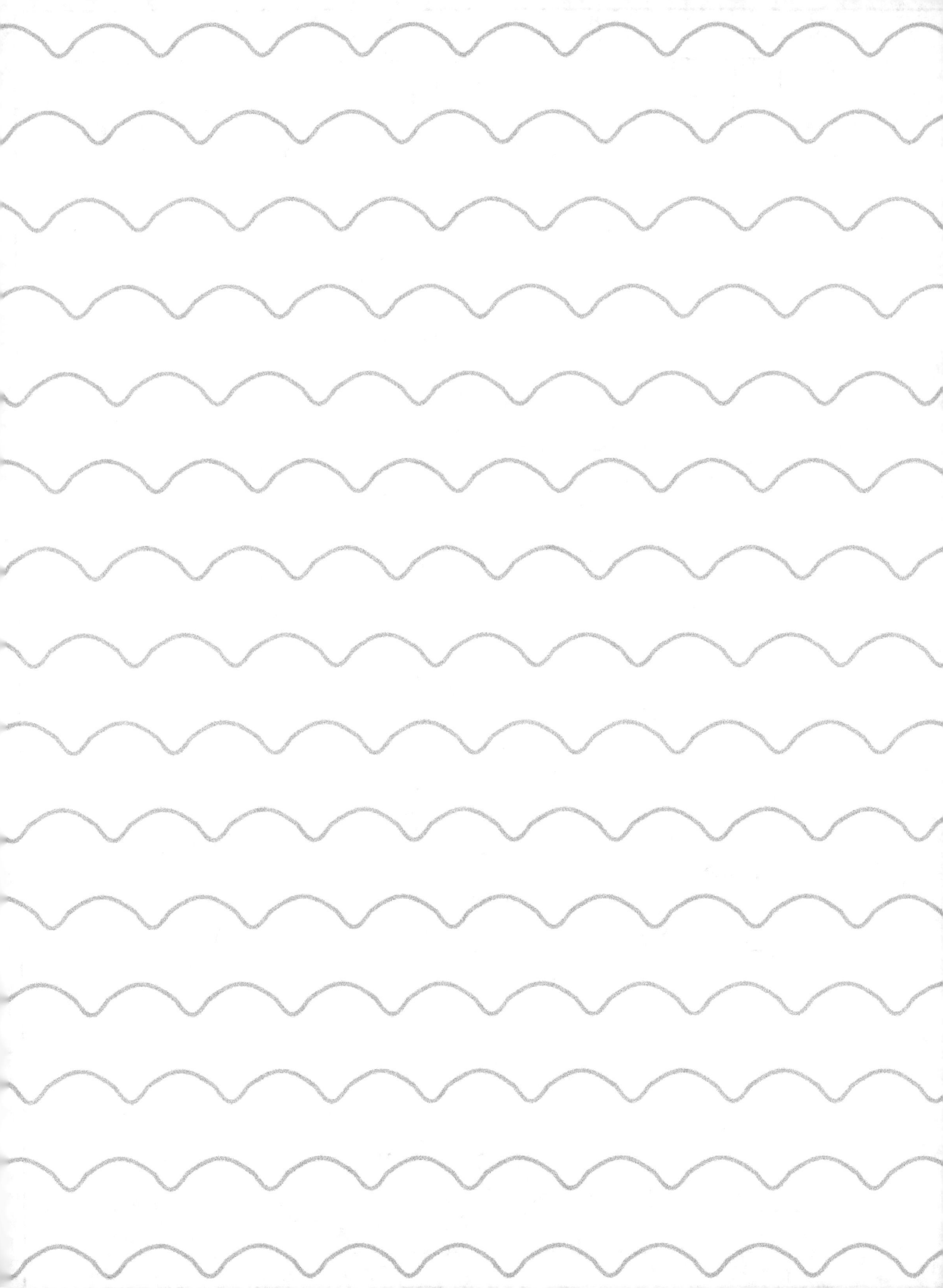

CANADA

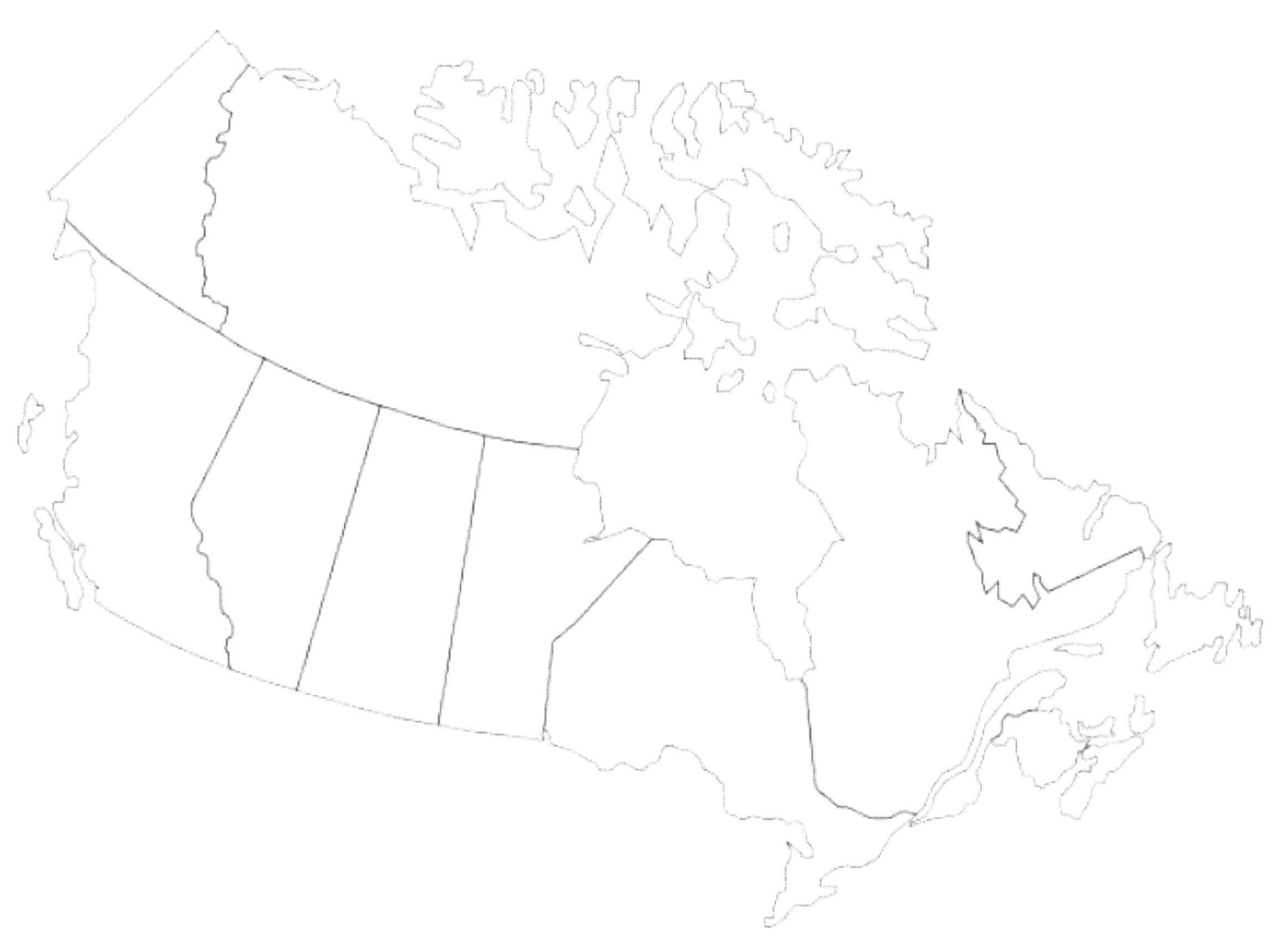

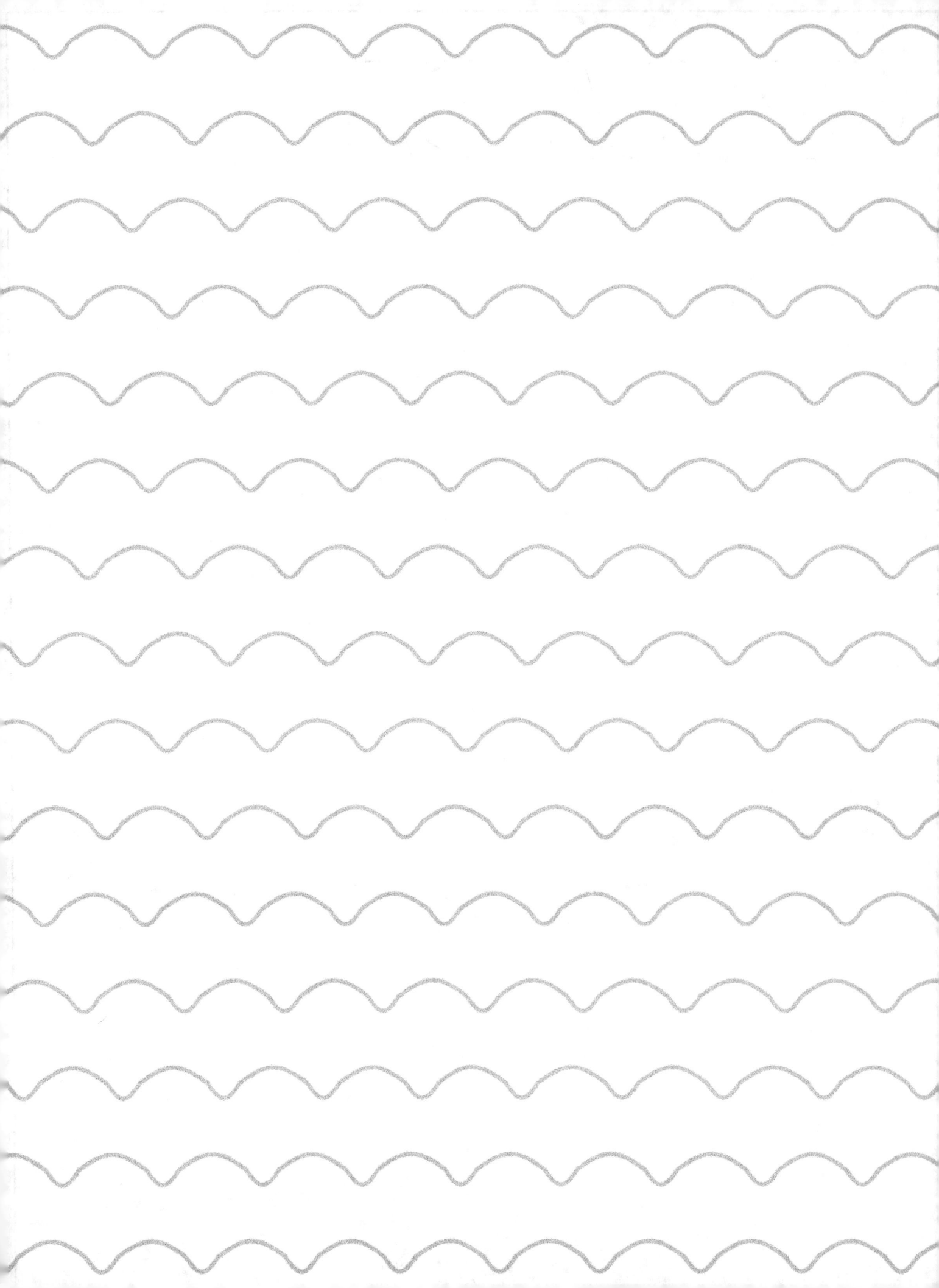

DENMARK

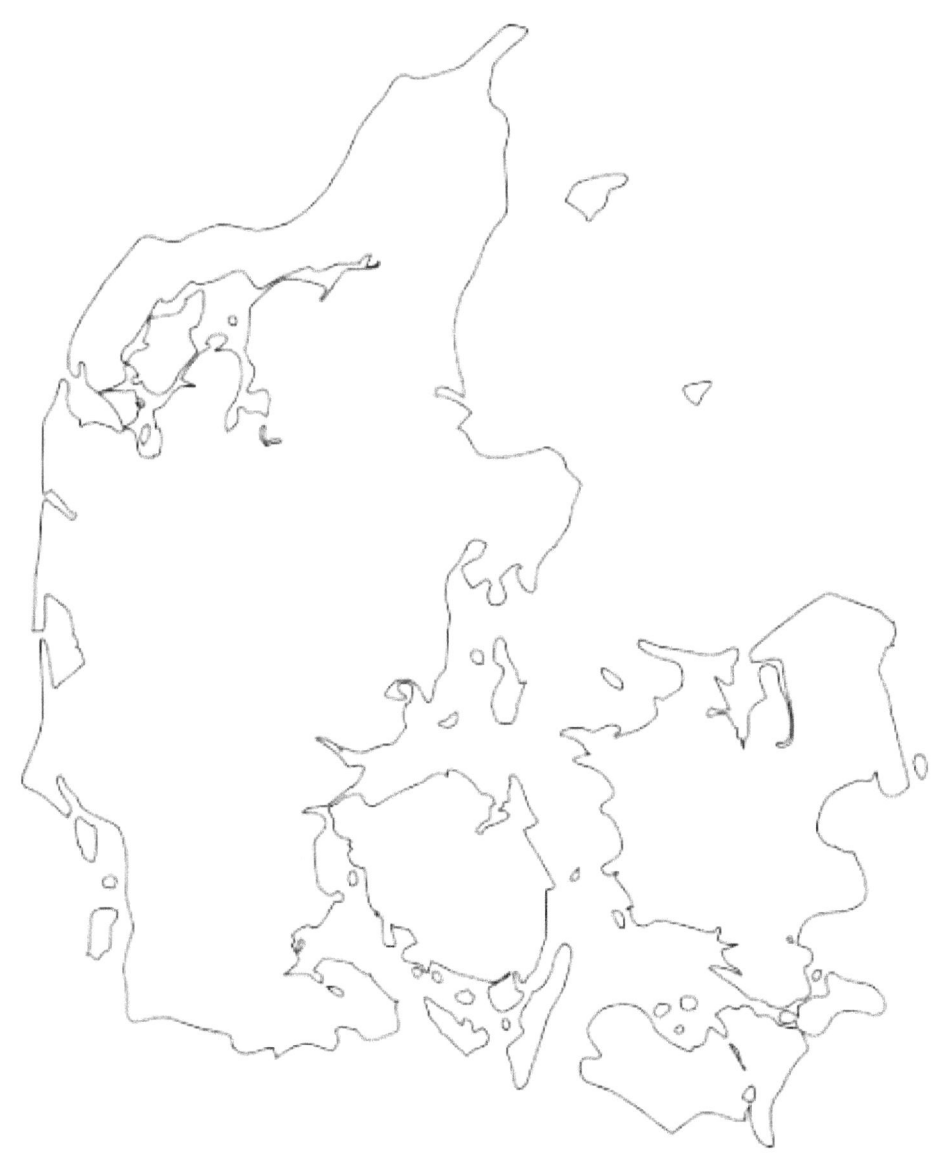

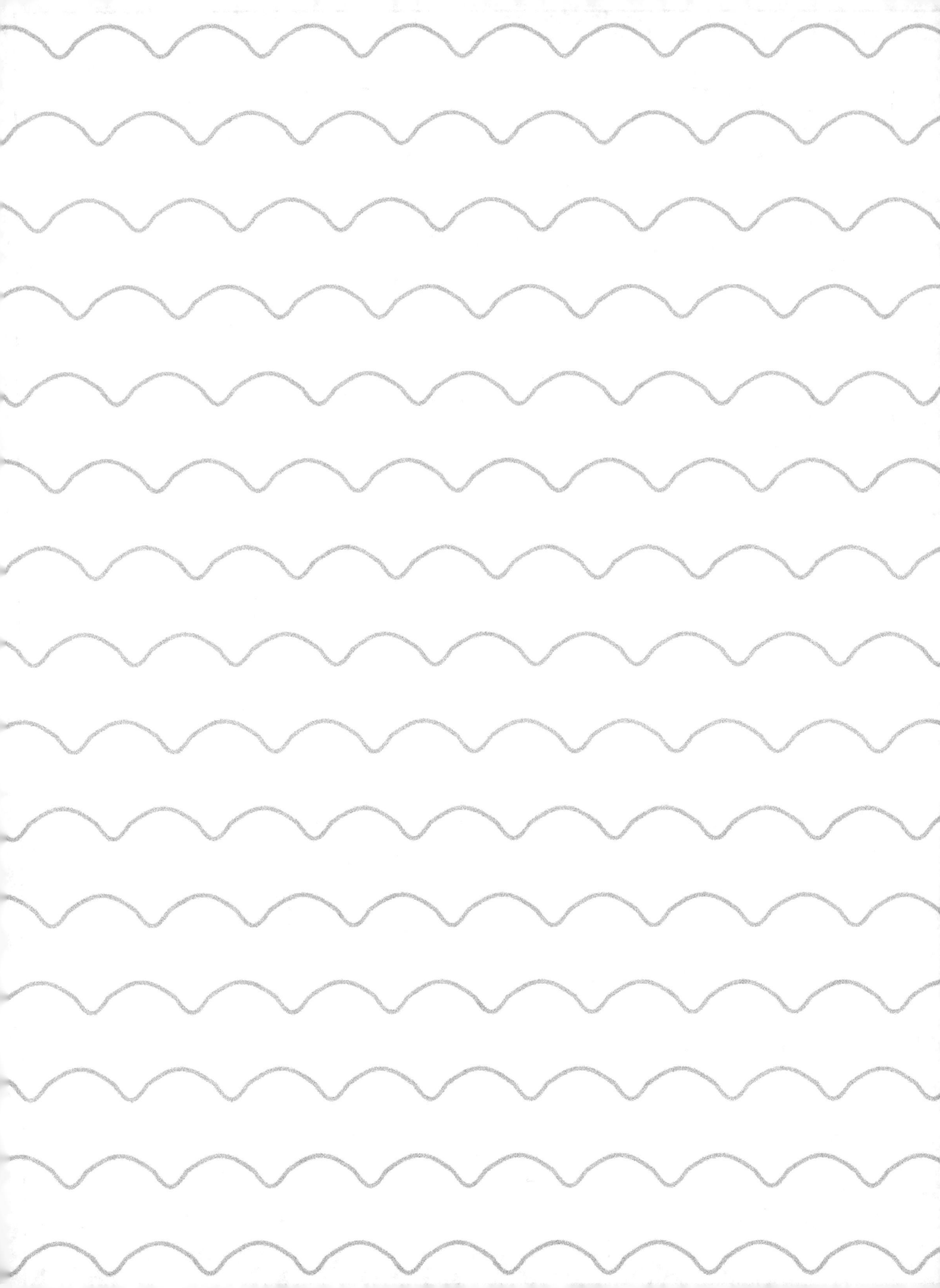

EASTERN U.S.

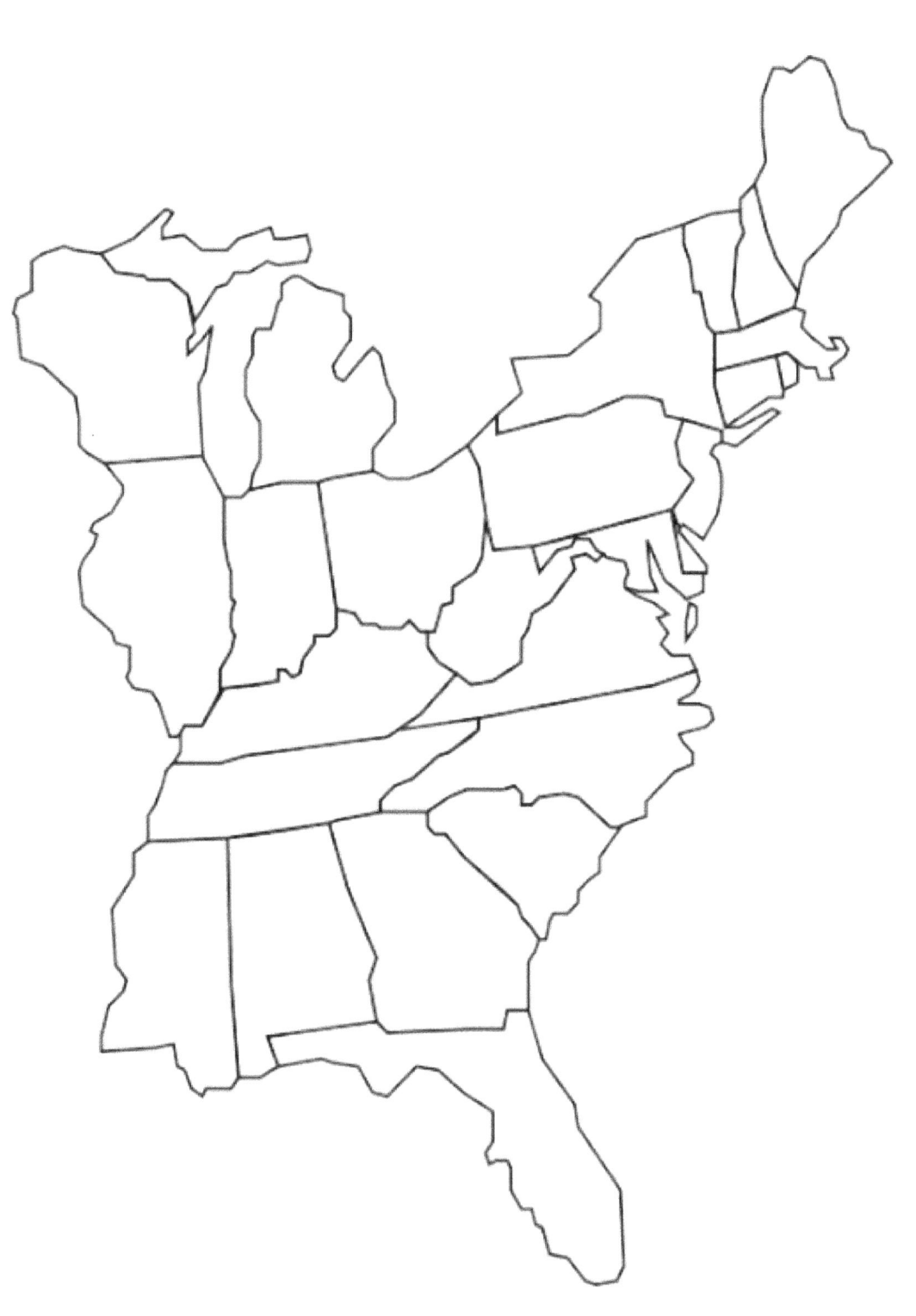

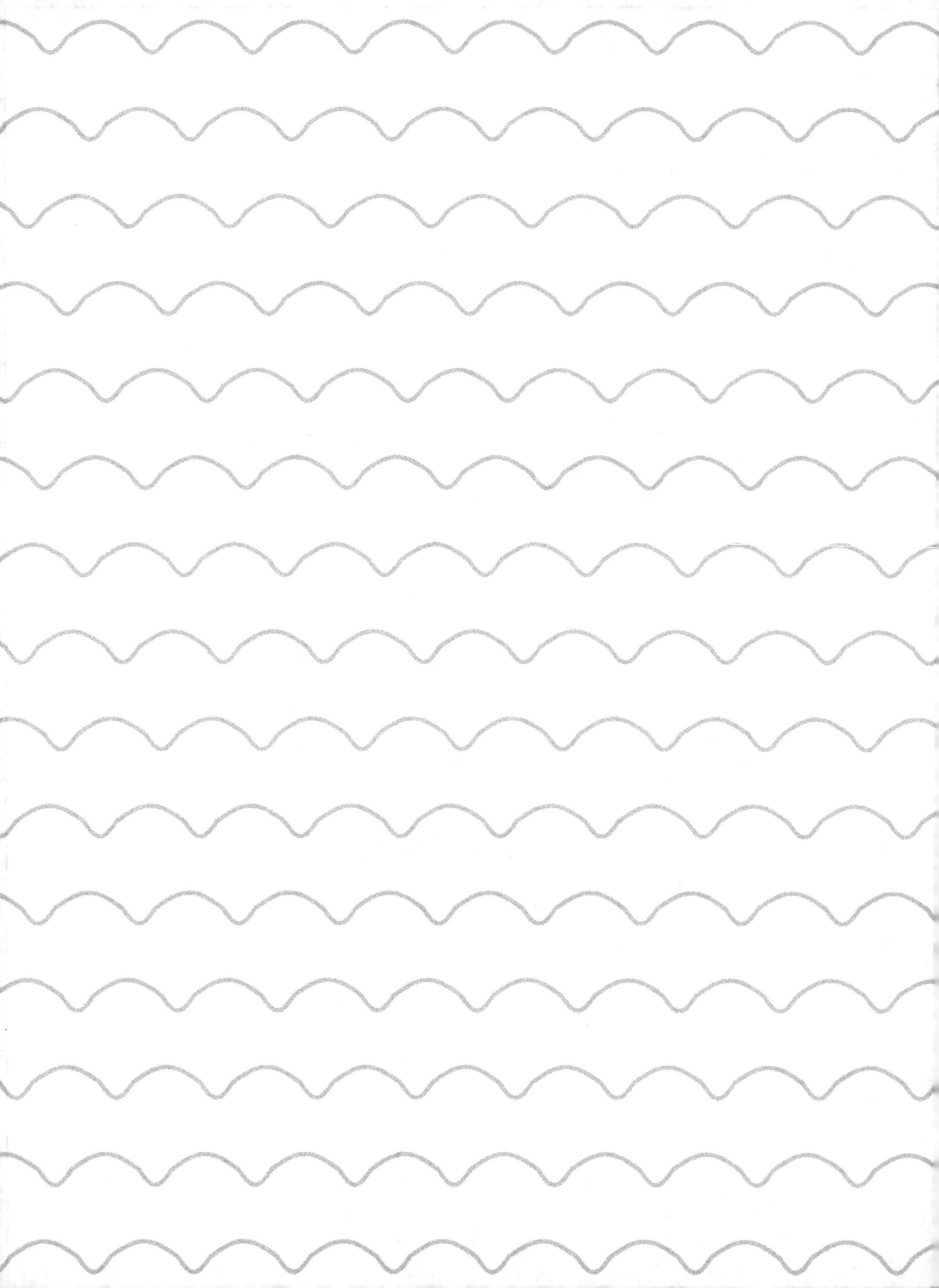

EUROPE

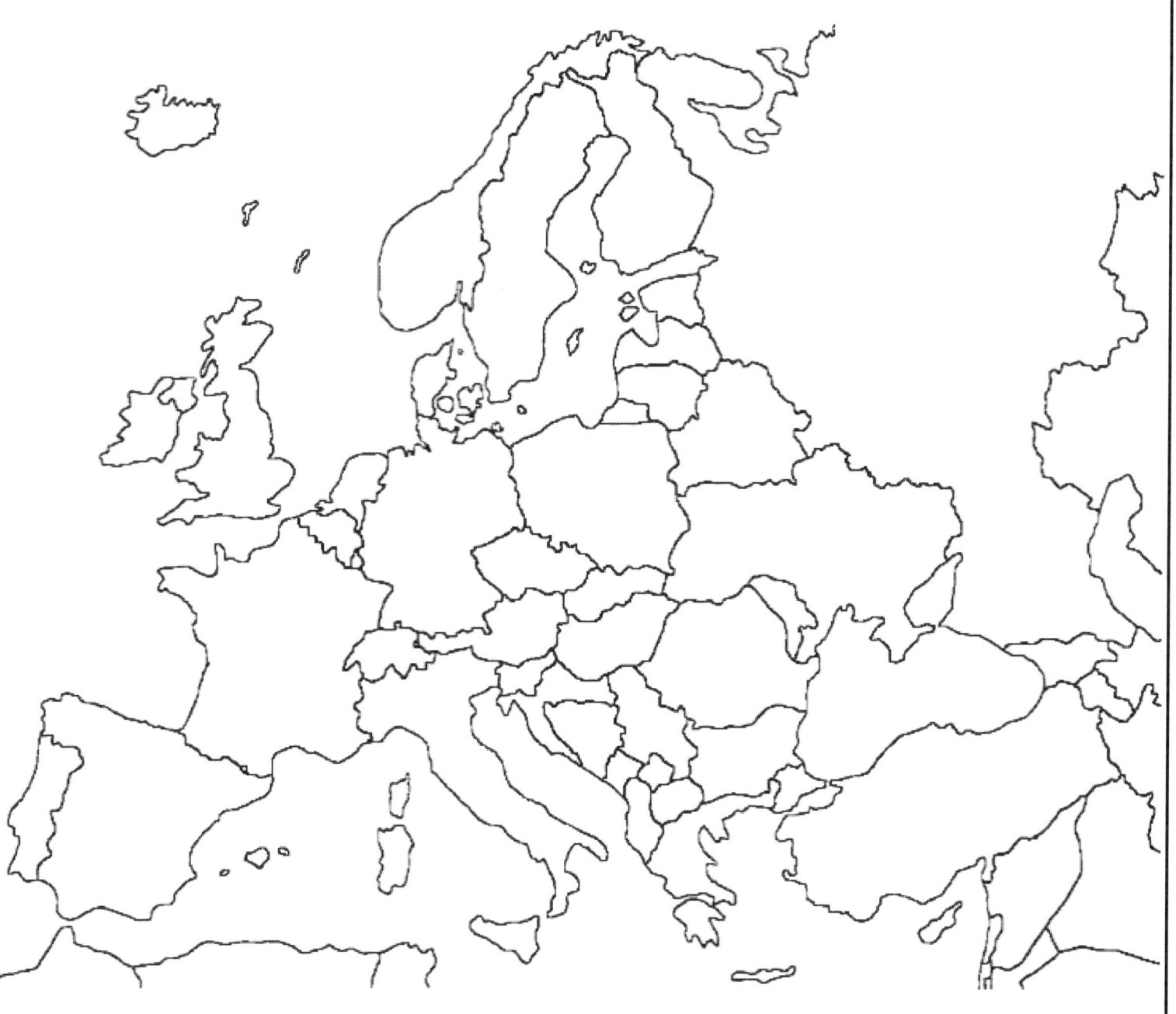

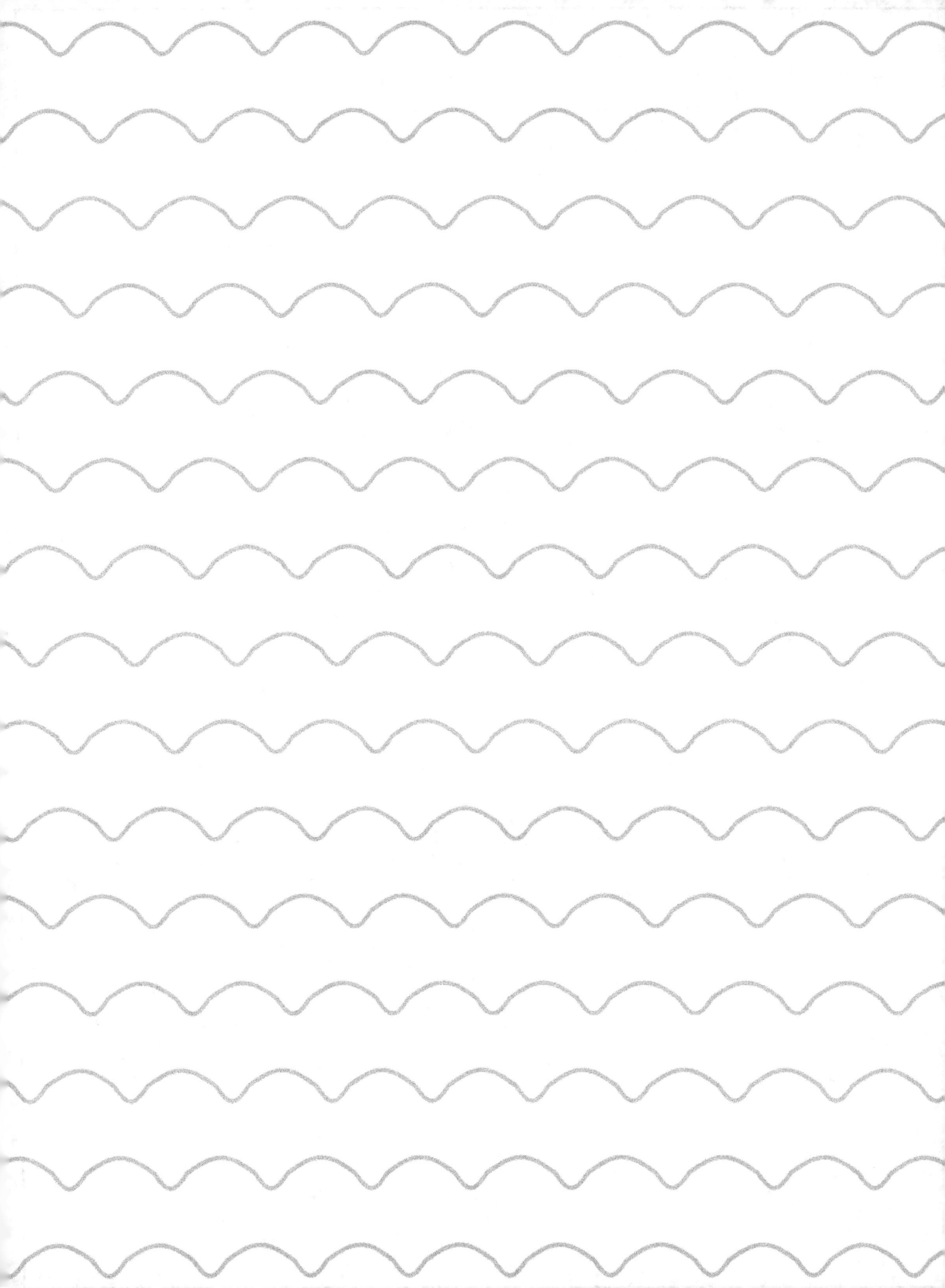

FRANCE

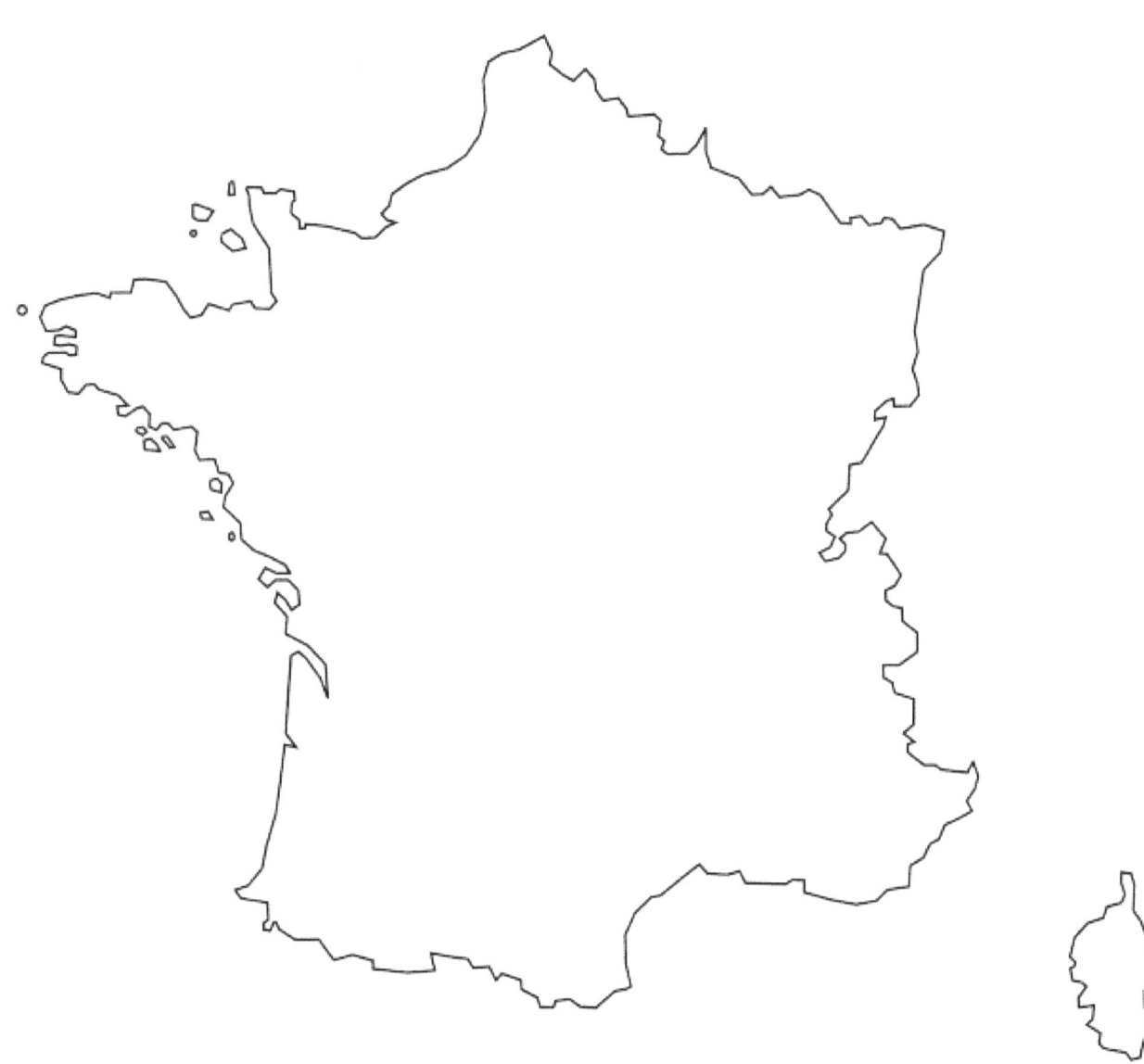

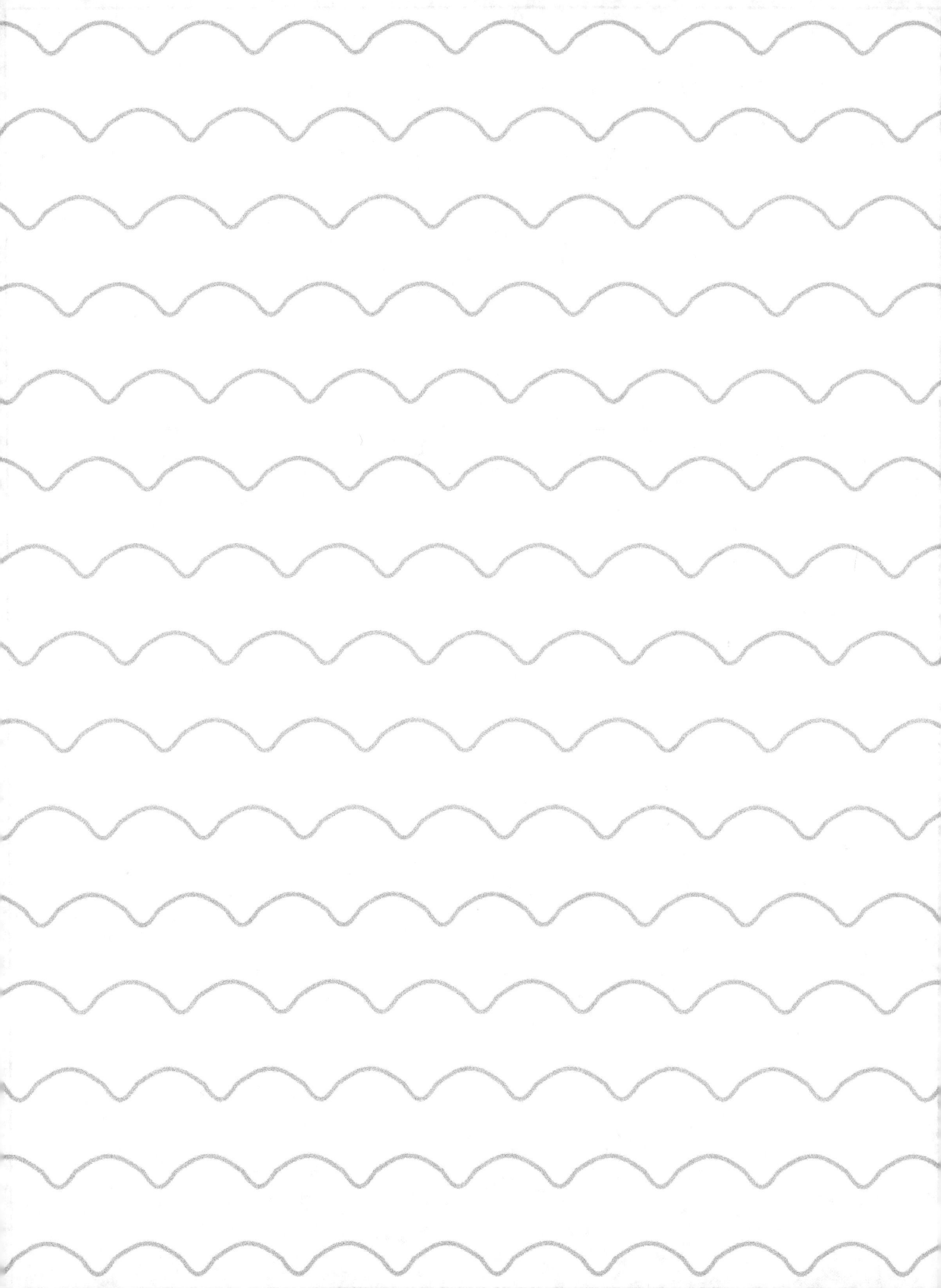

ICELAND

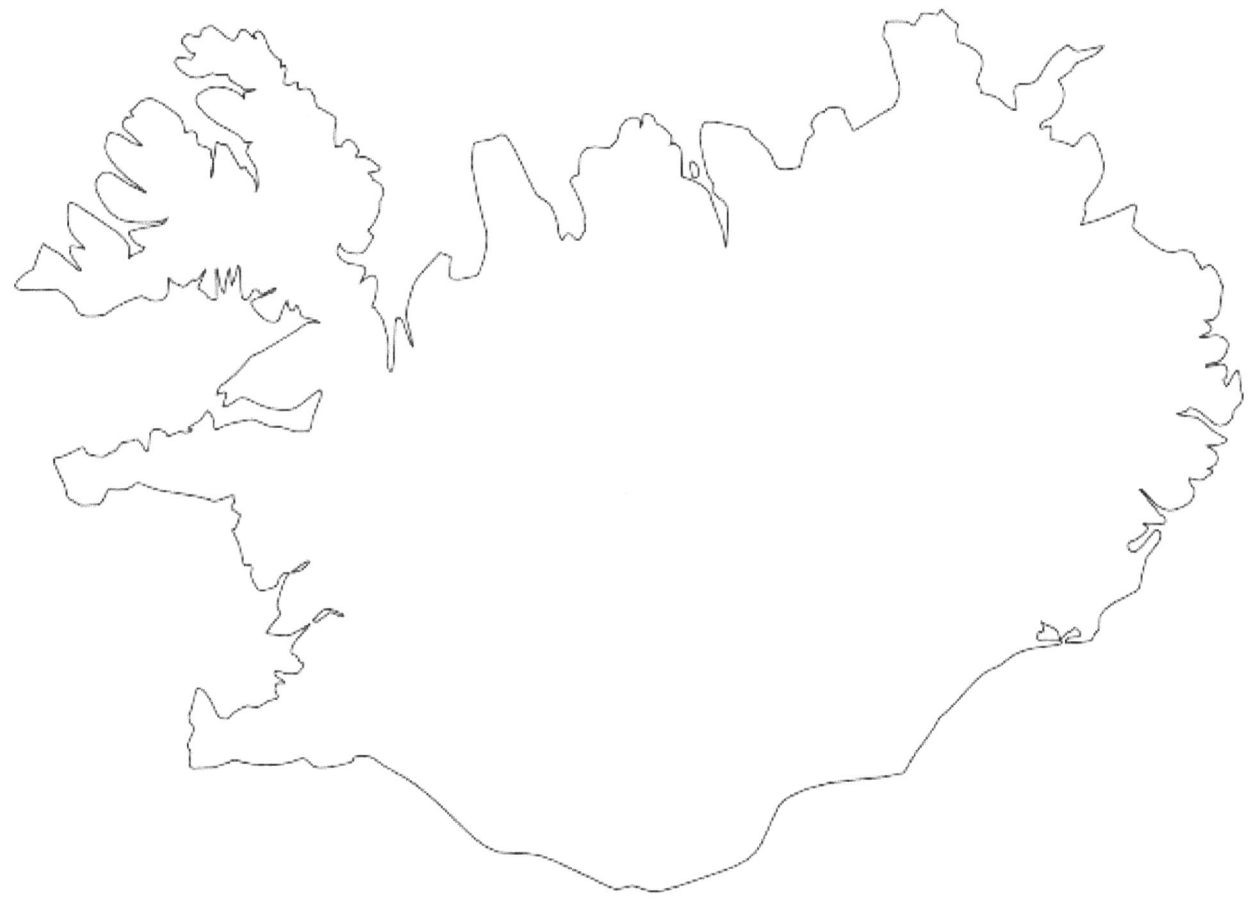

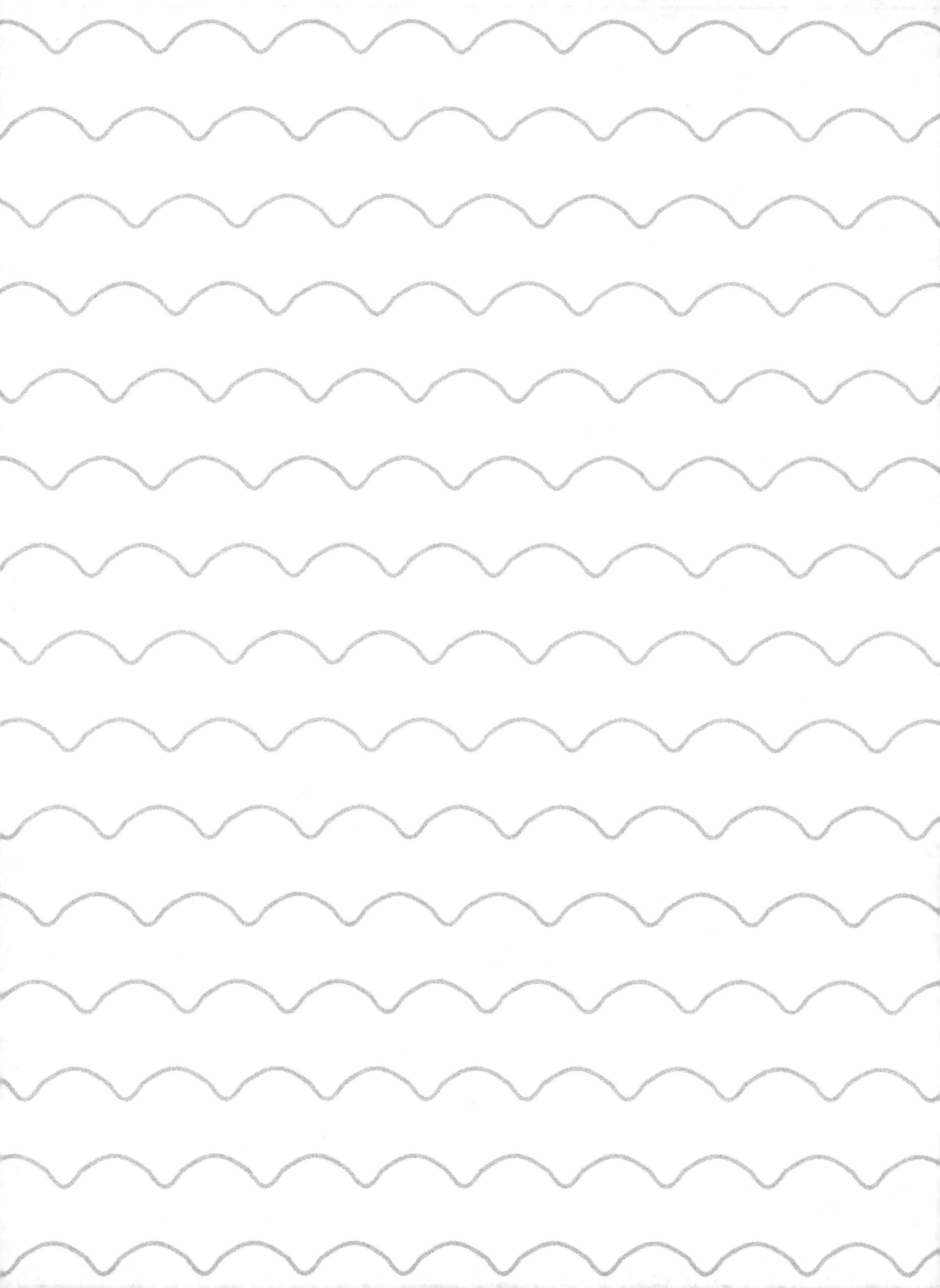

INDONESIA

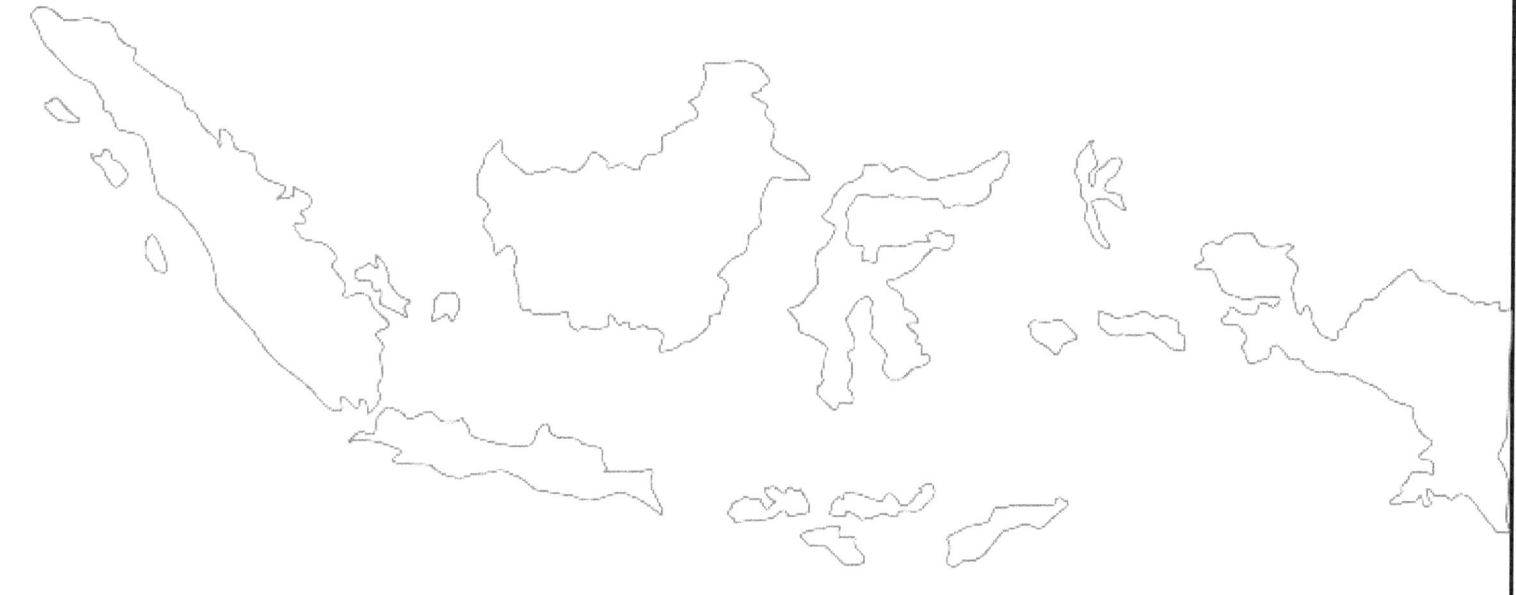

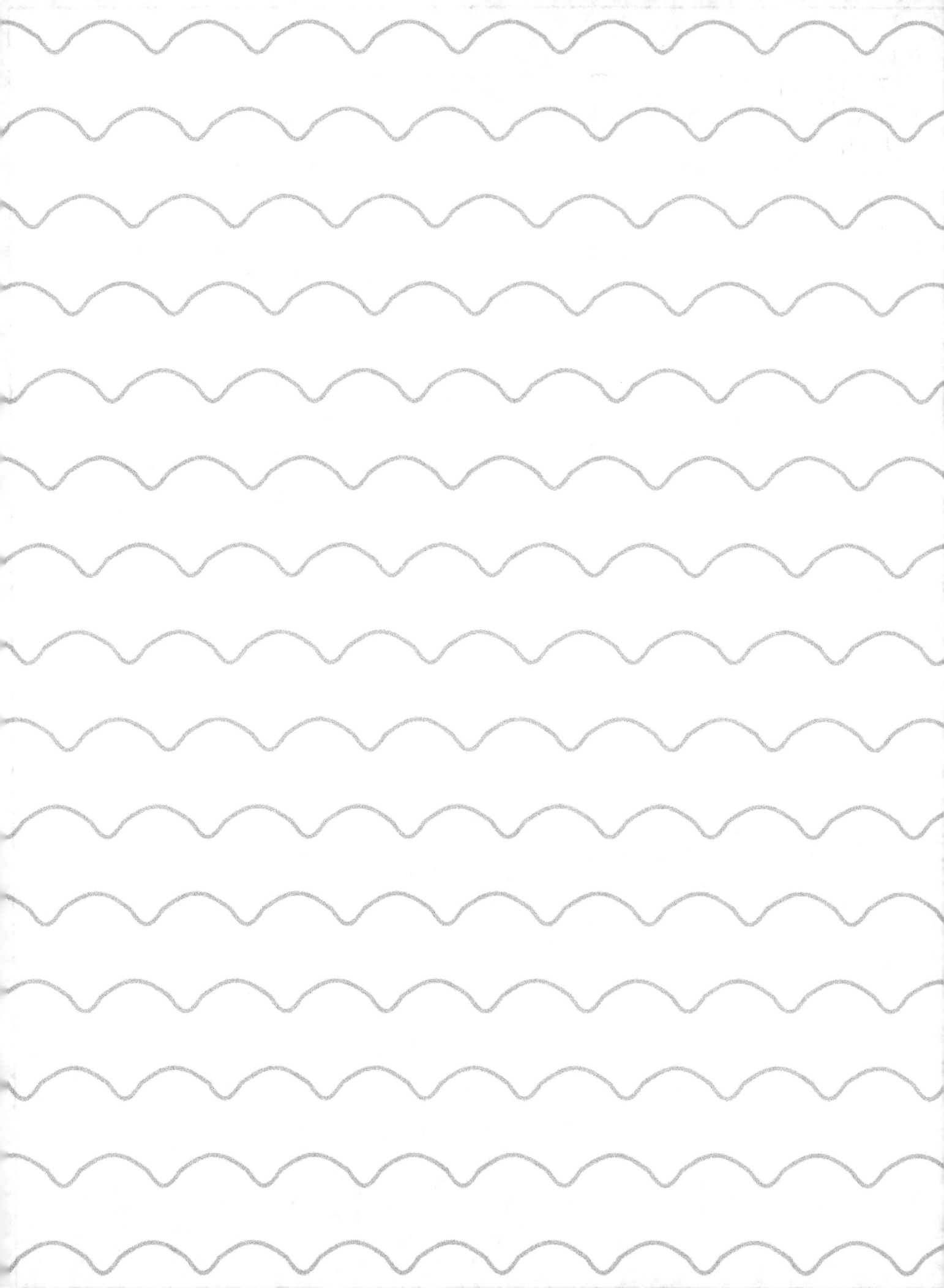

IRELAND

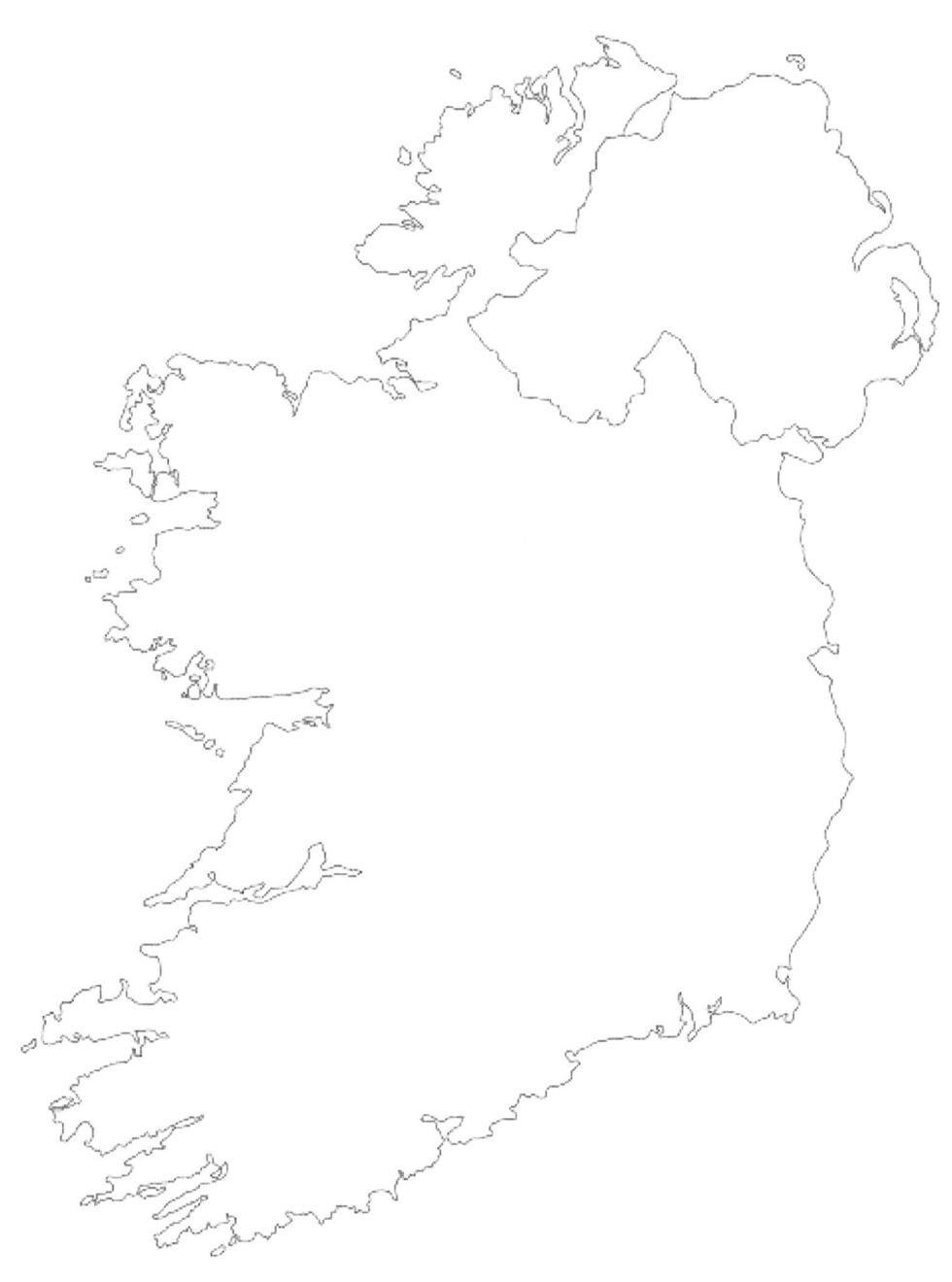

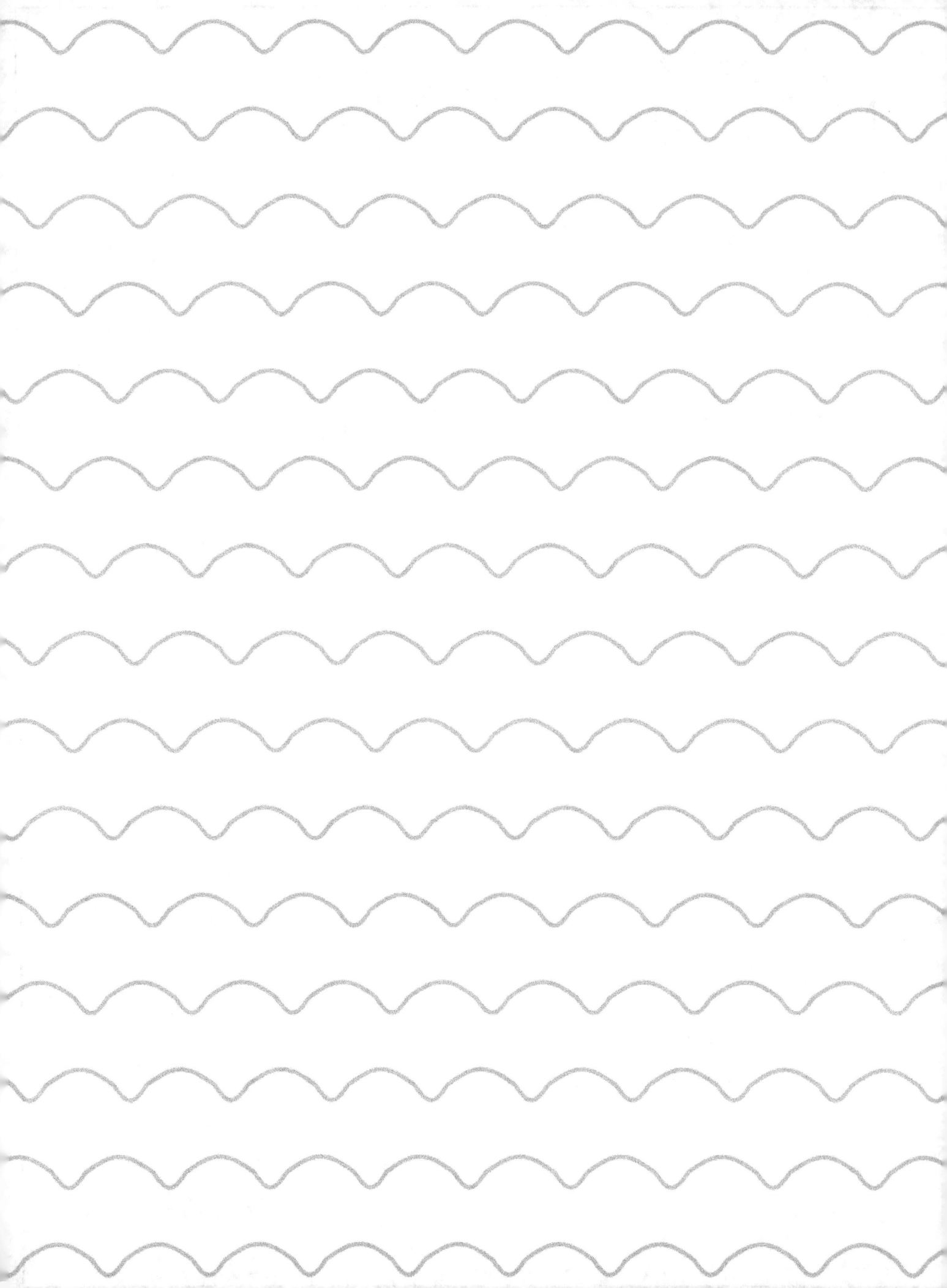

ITALY

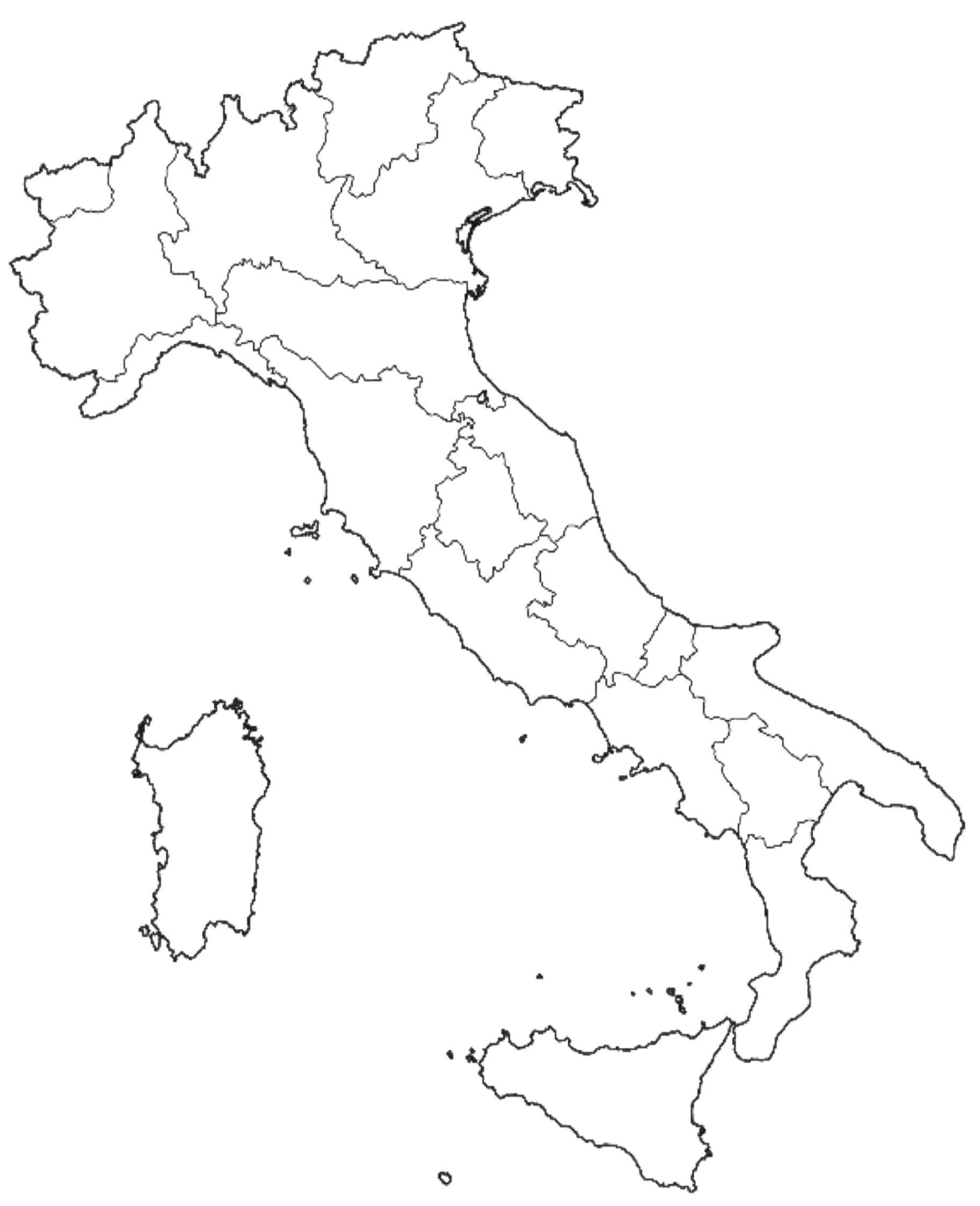

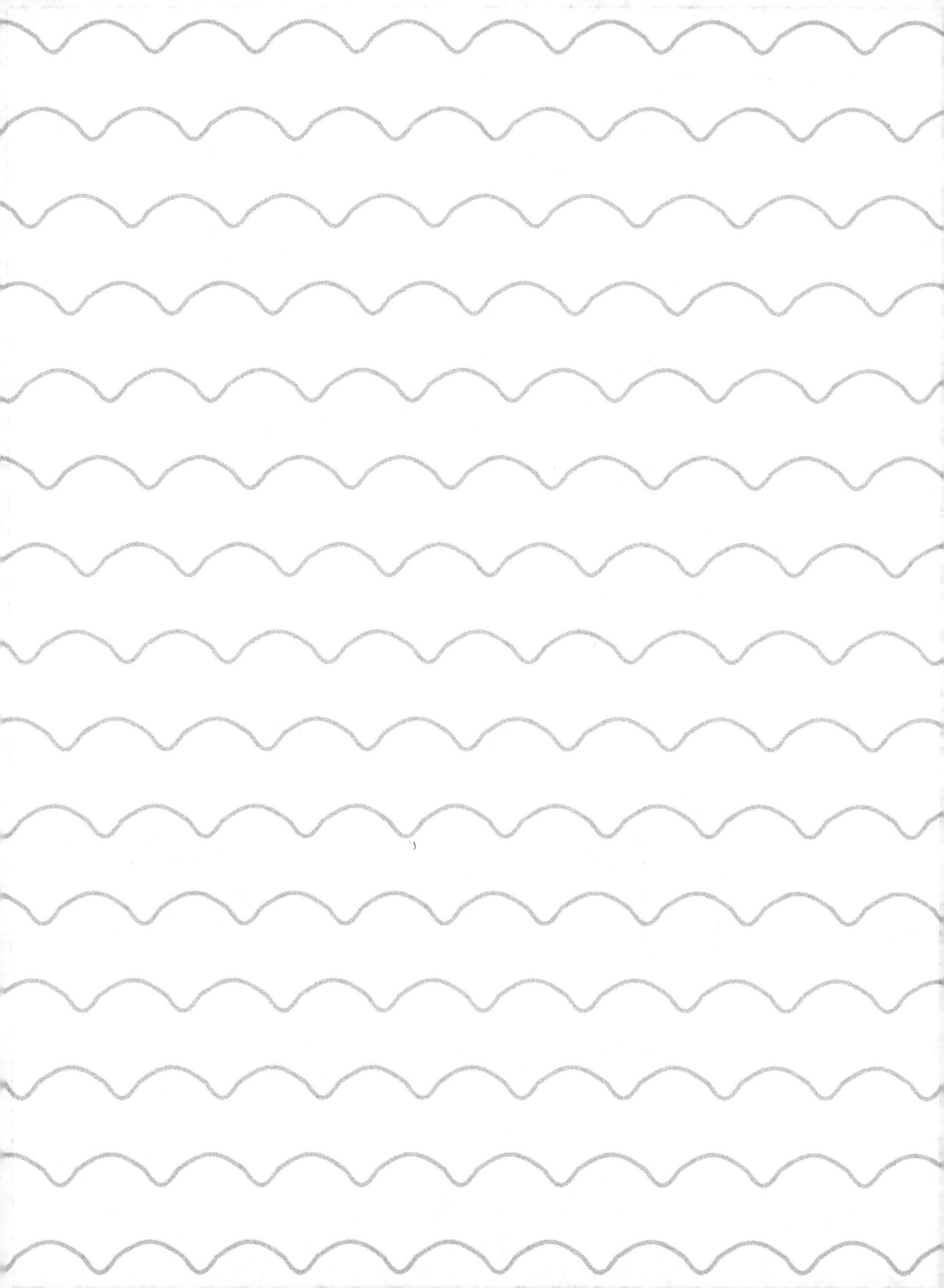

MEXICO

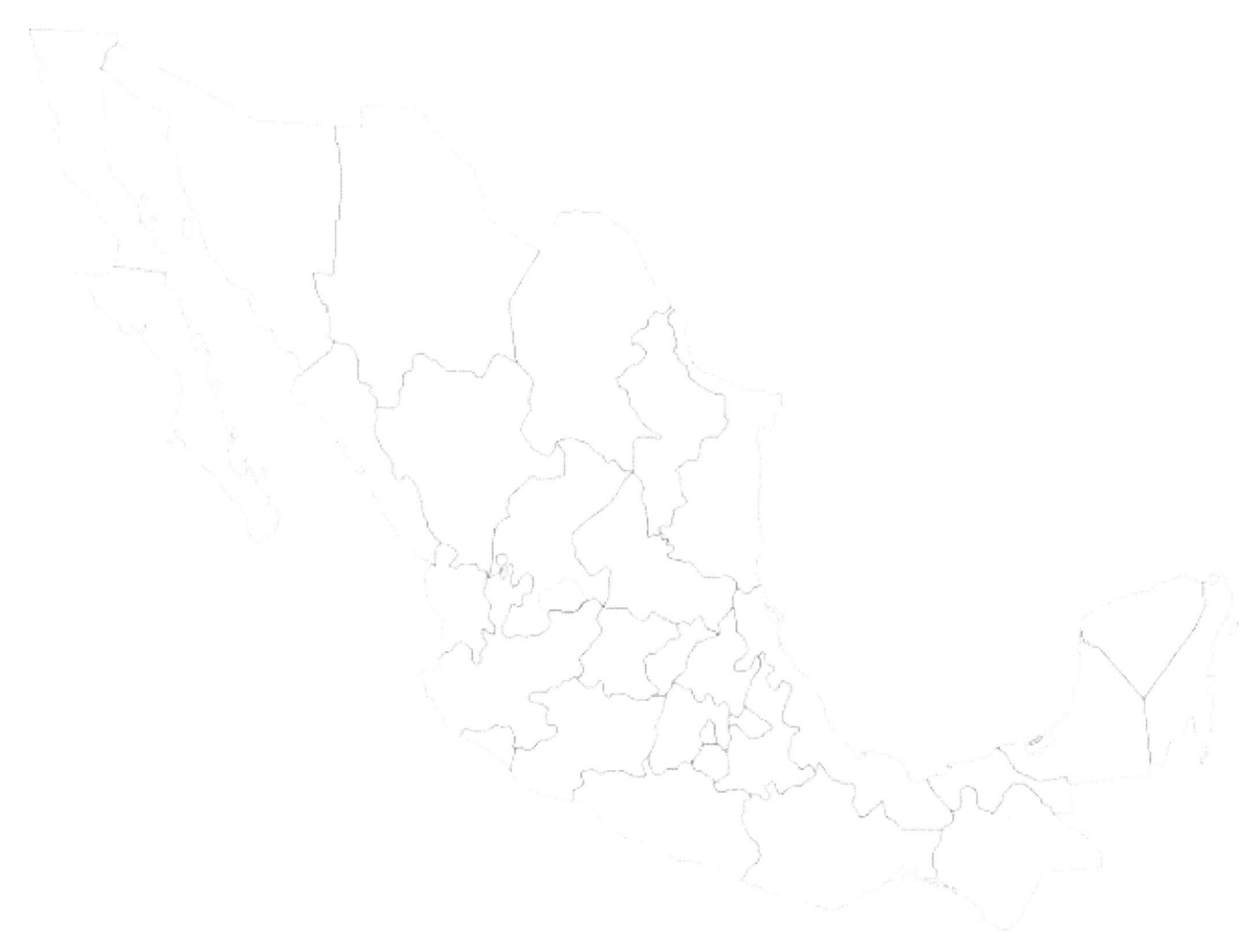

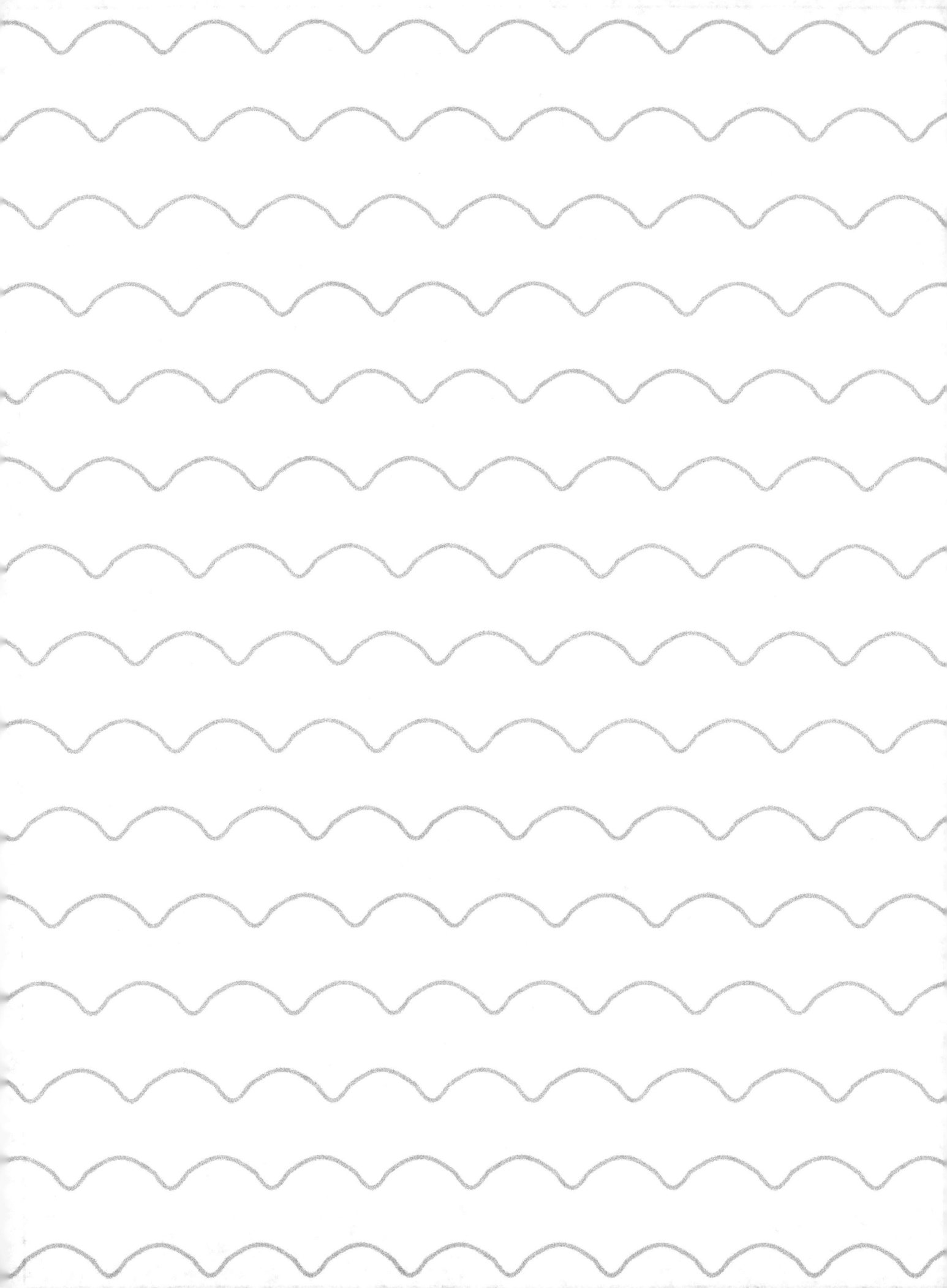

THE MIDDLE

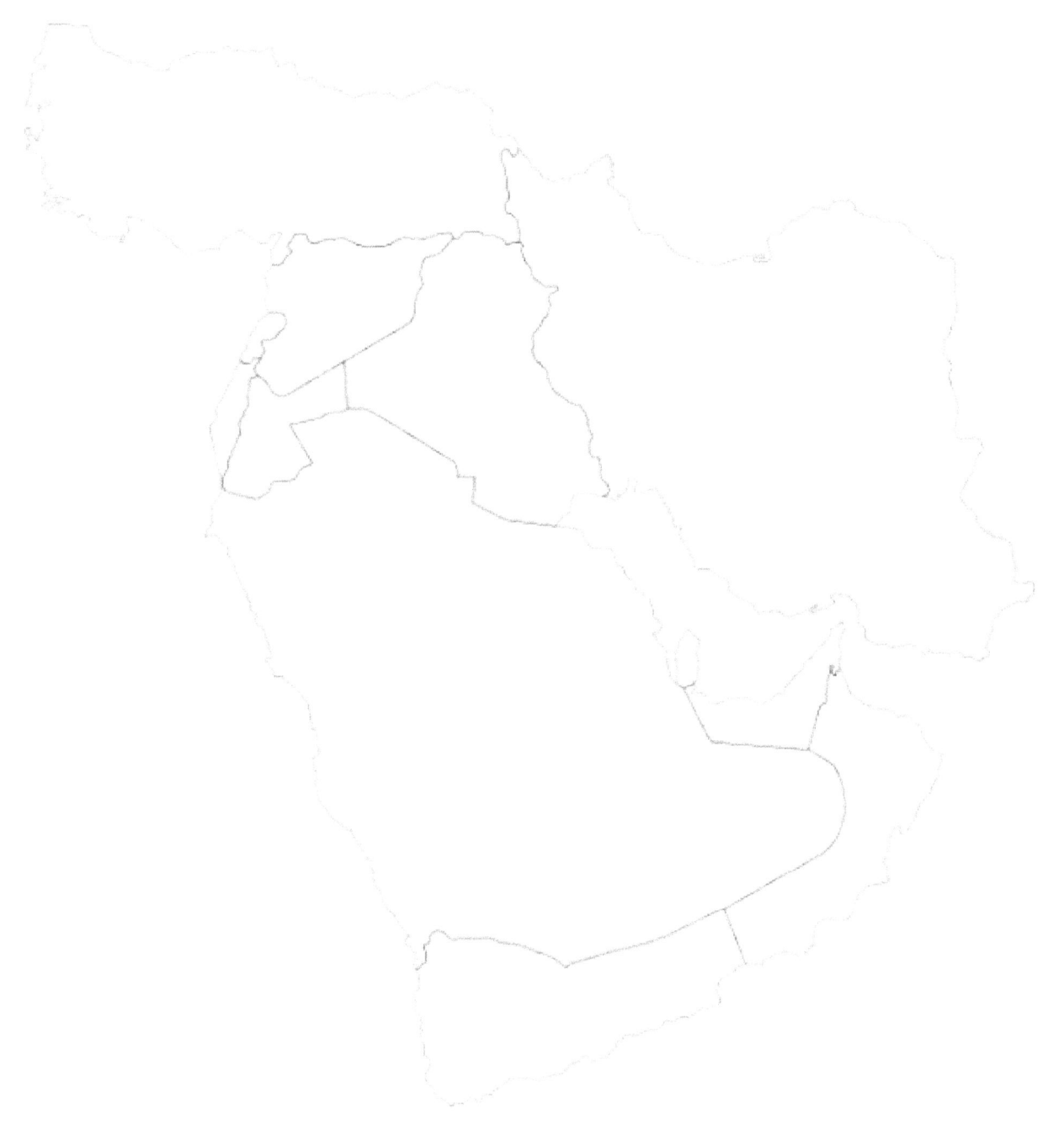

EAST

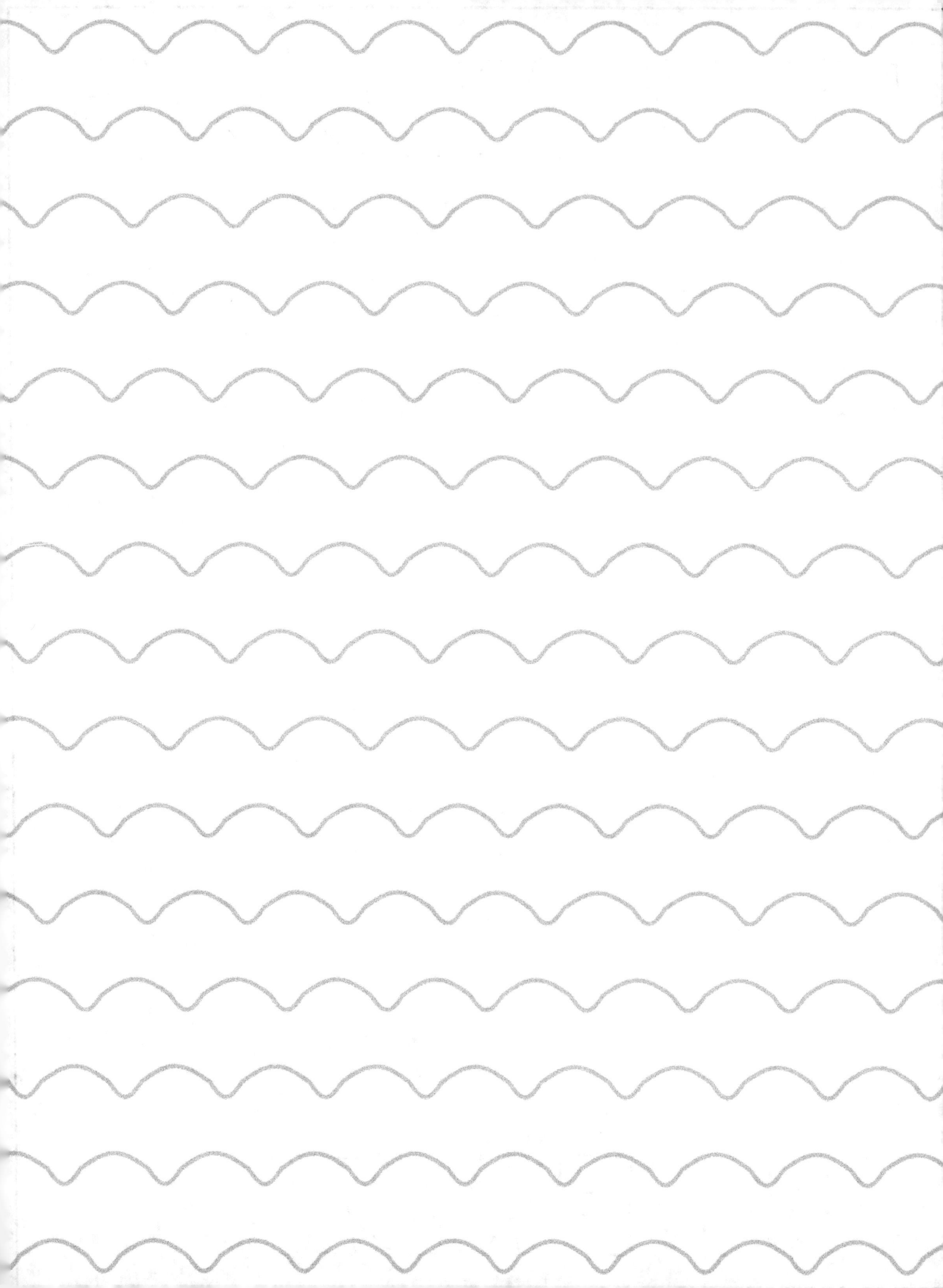

SCOTLAND

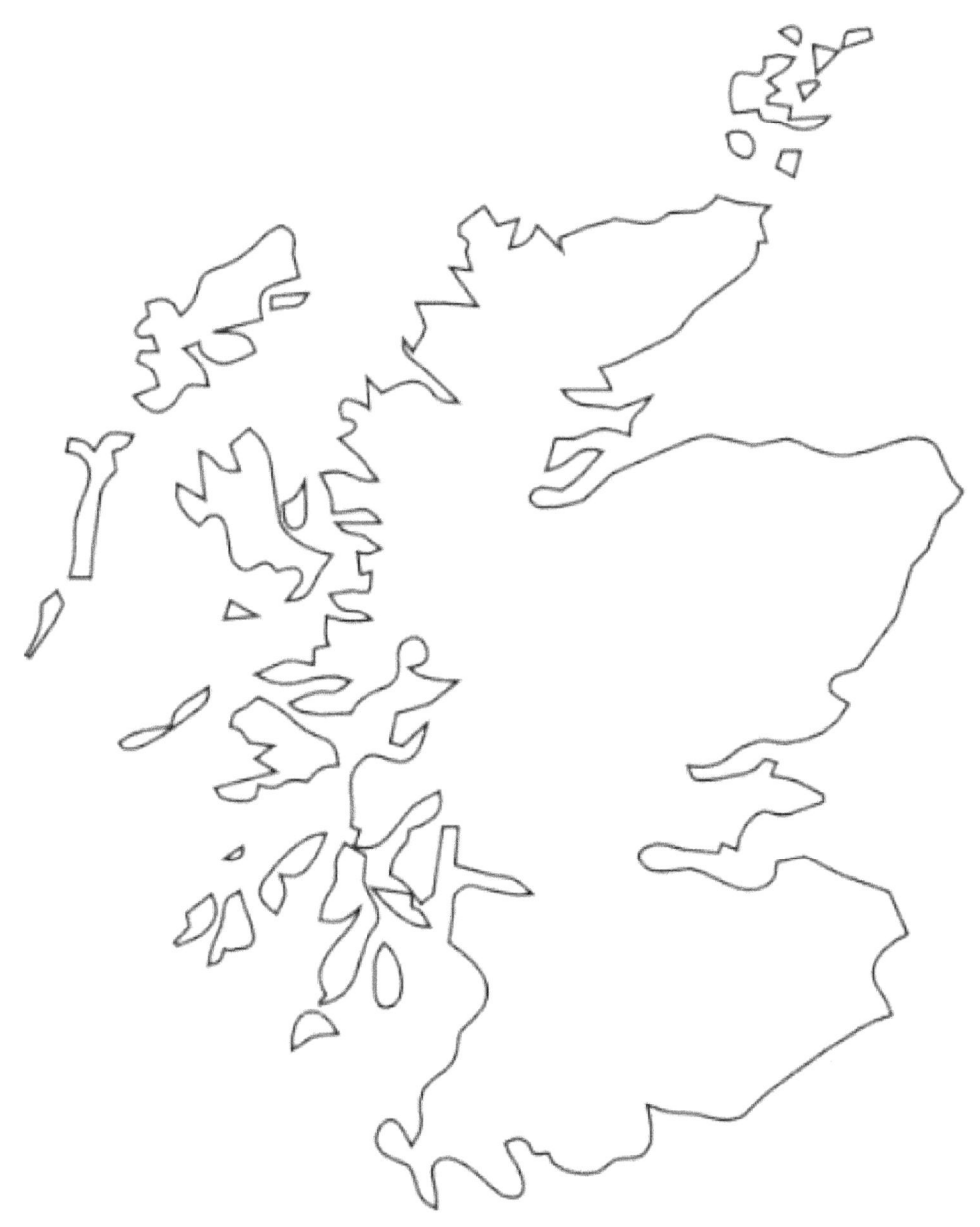

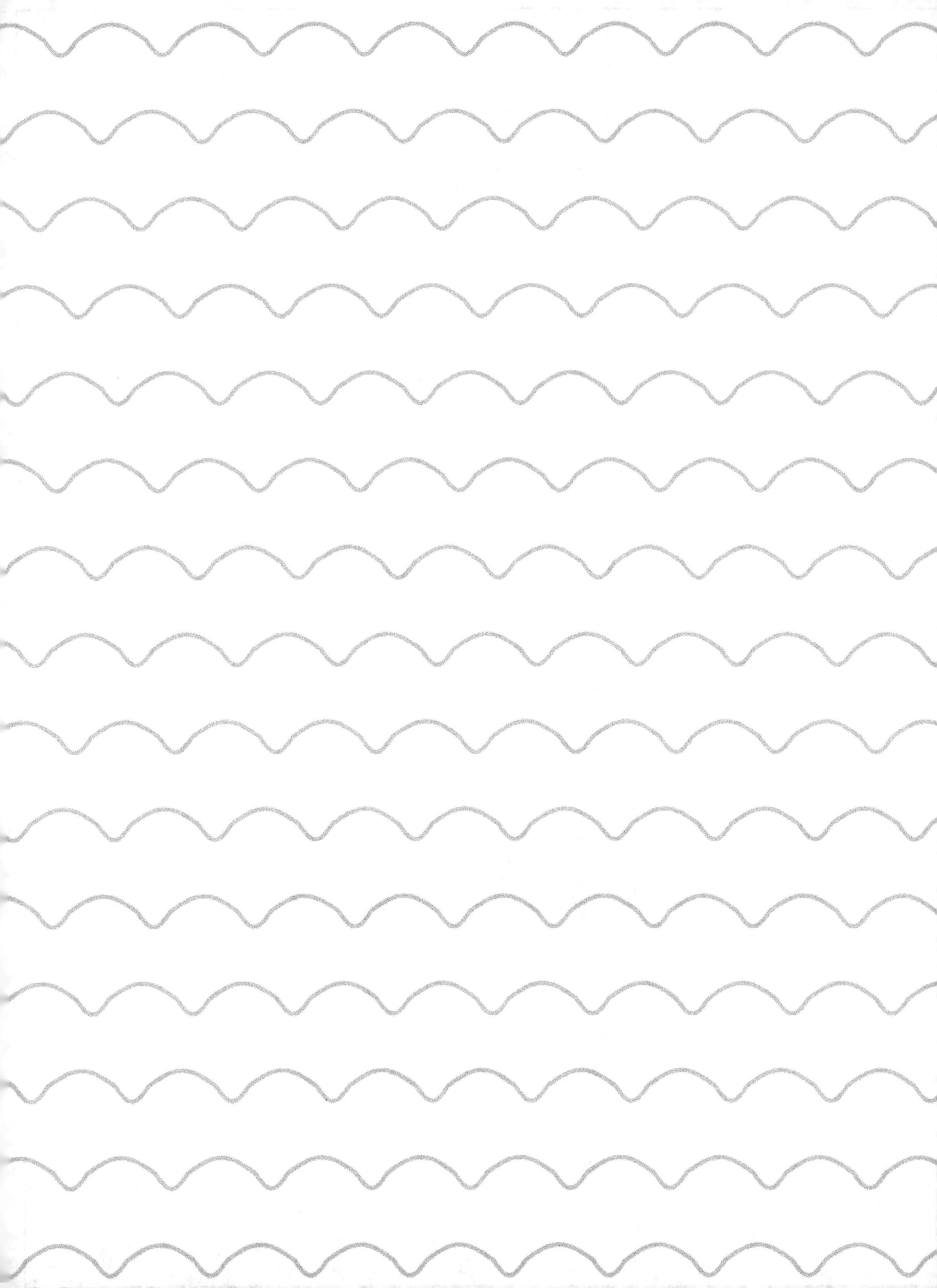

SOUTH

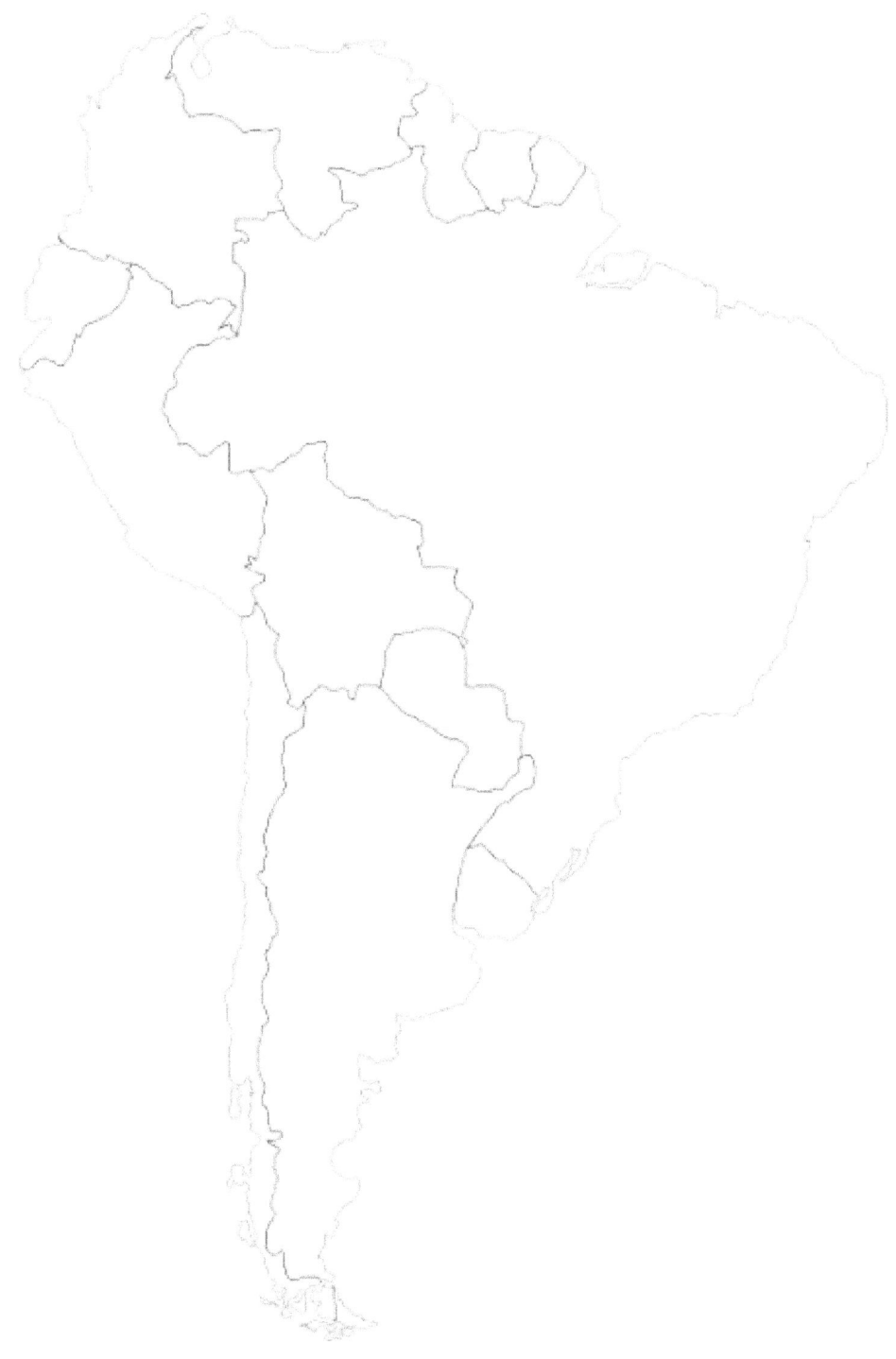

AMERICA

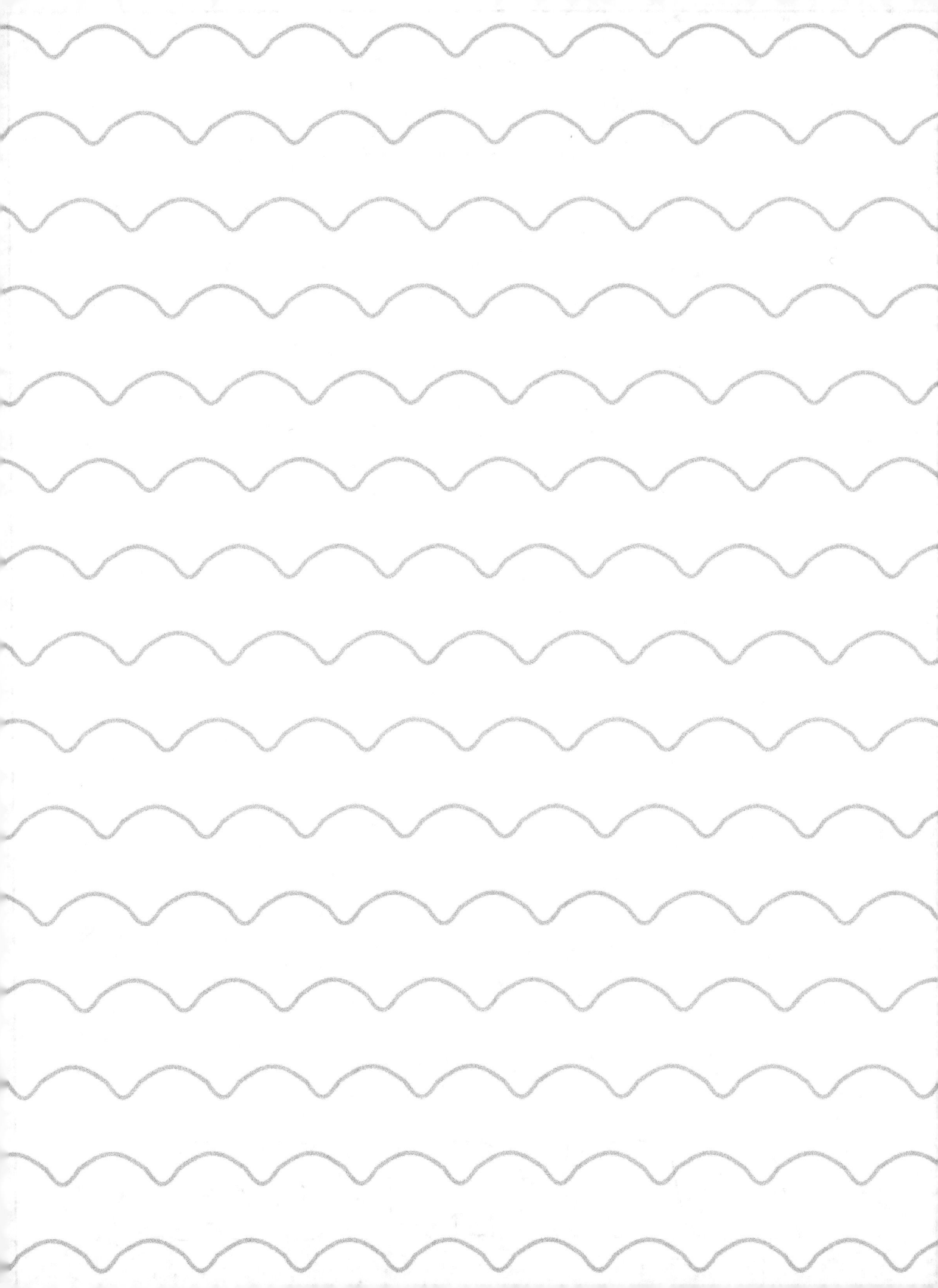

THE UNITED STATES

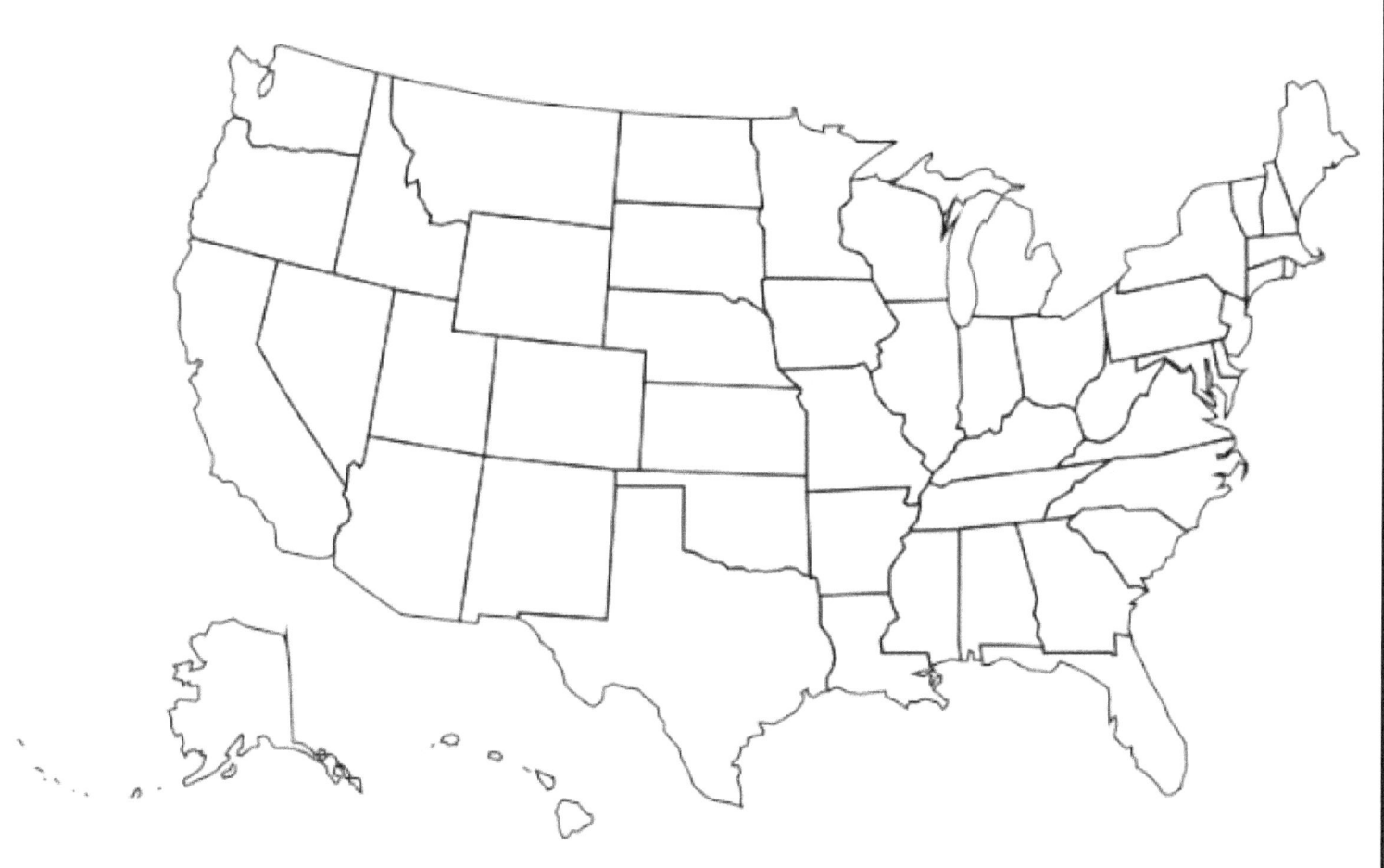

OF AMERICA

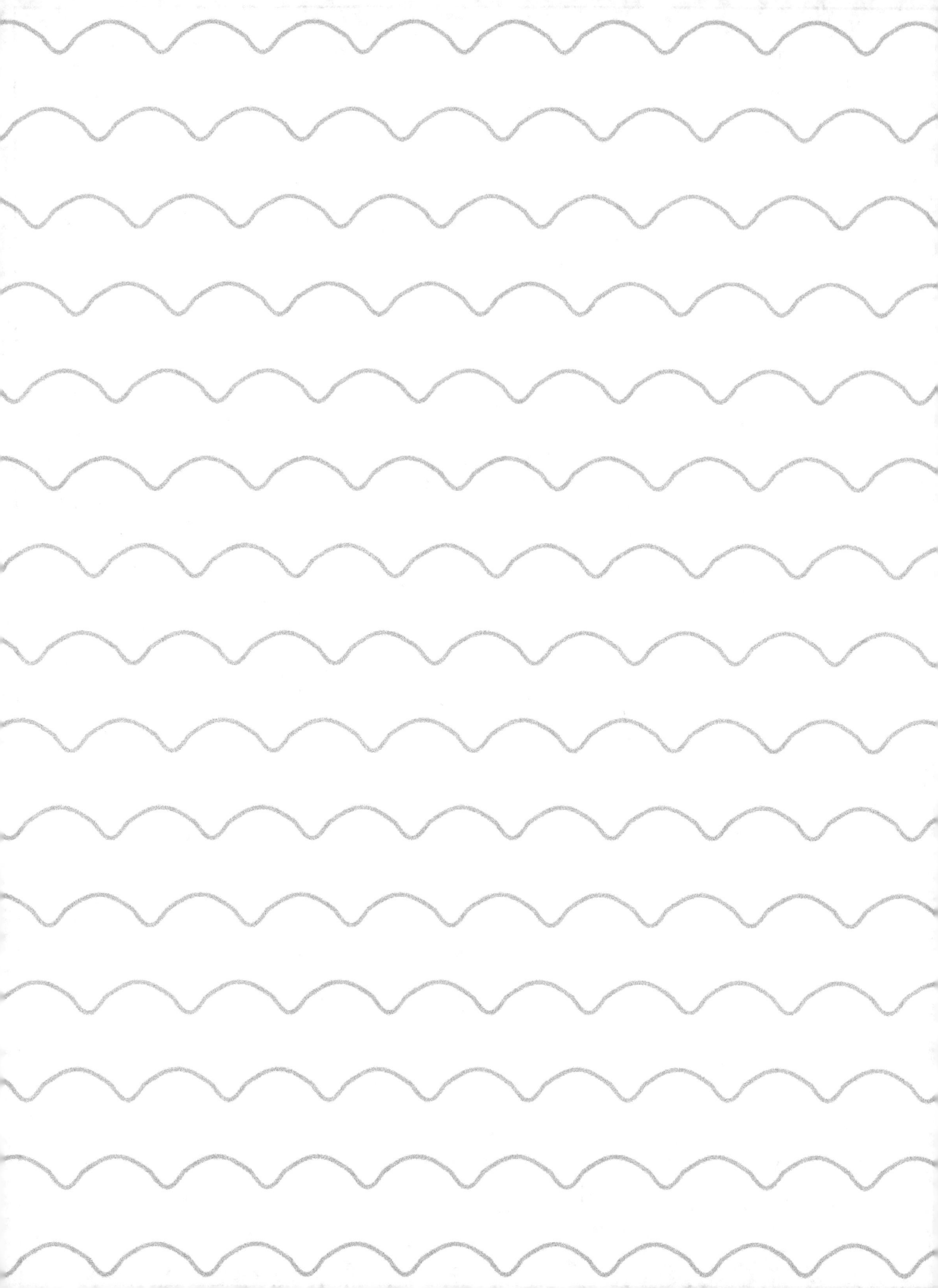

THE

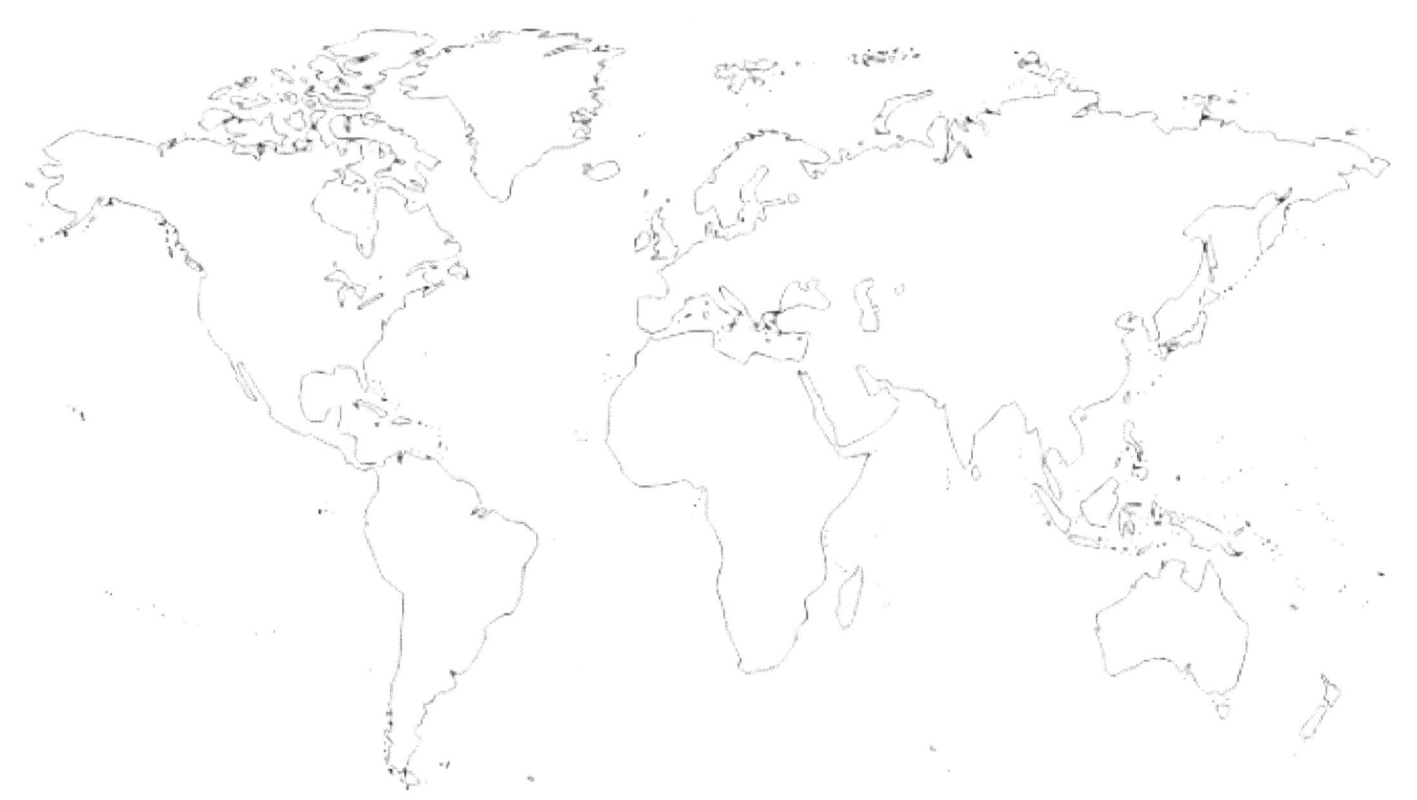

WORLD

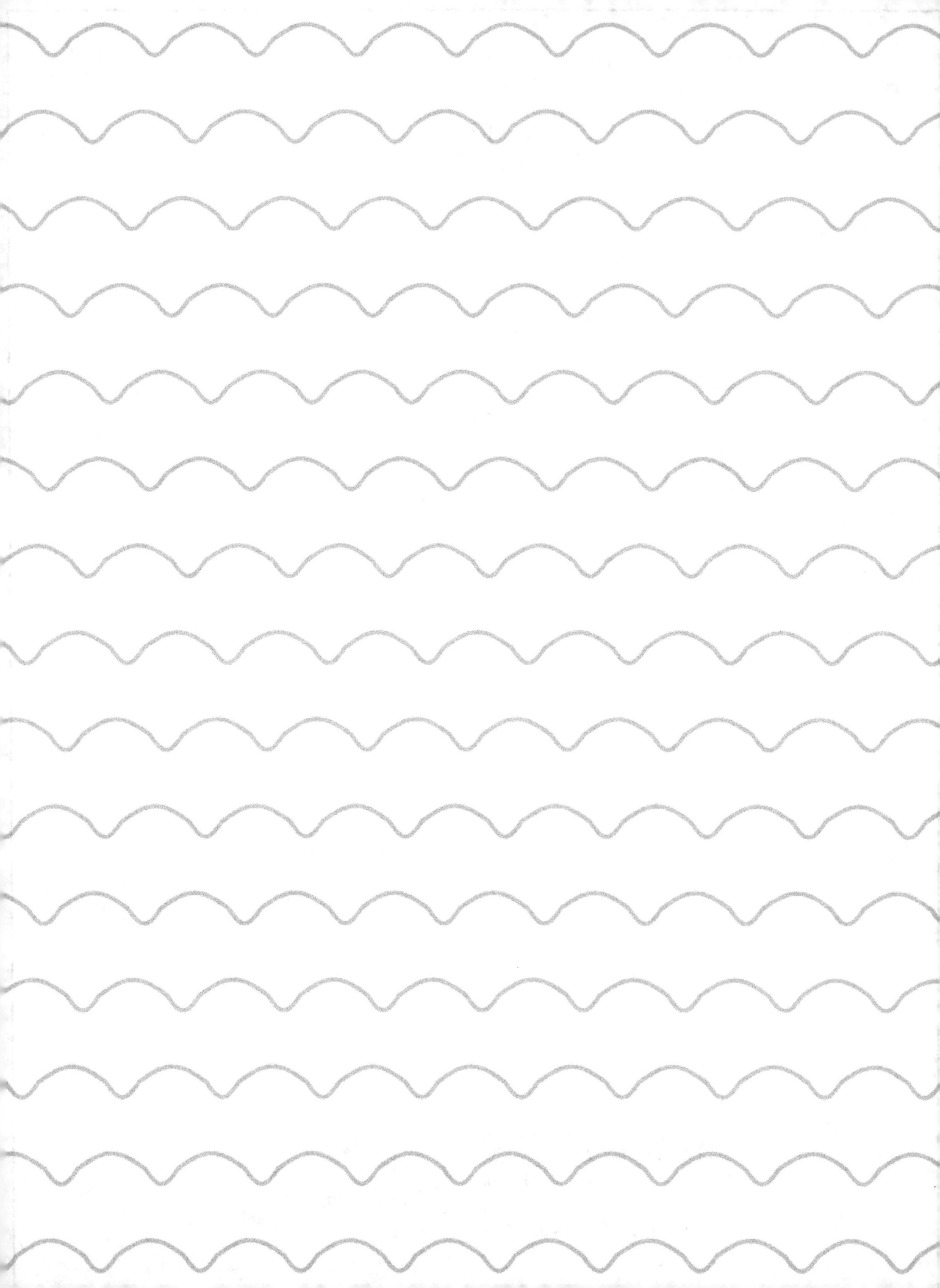

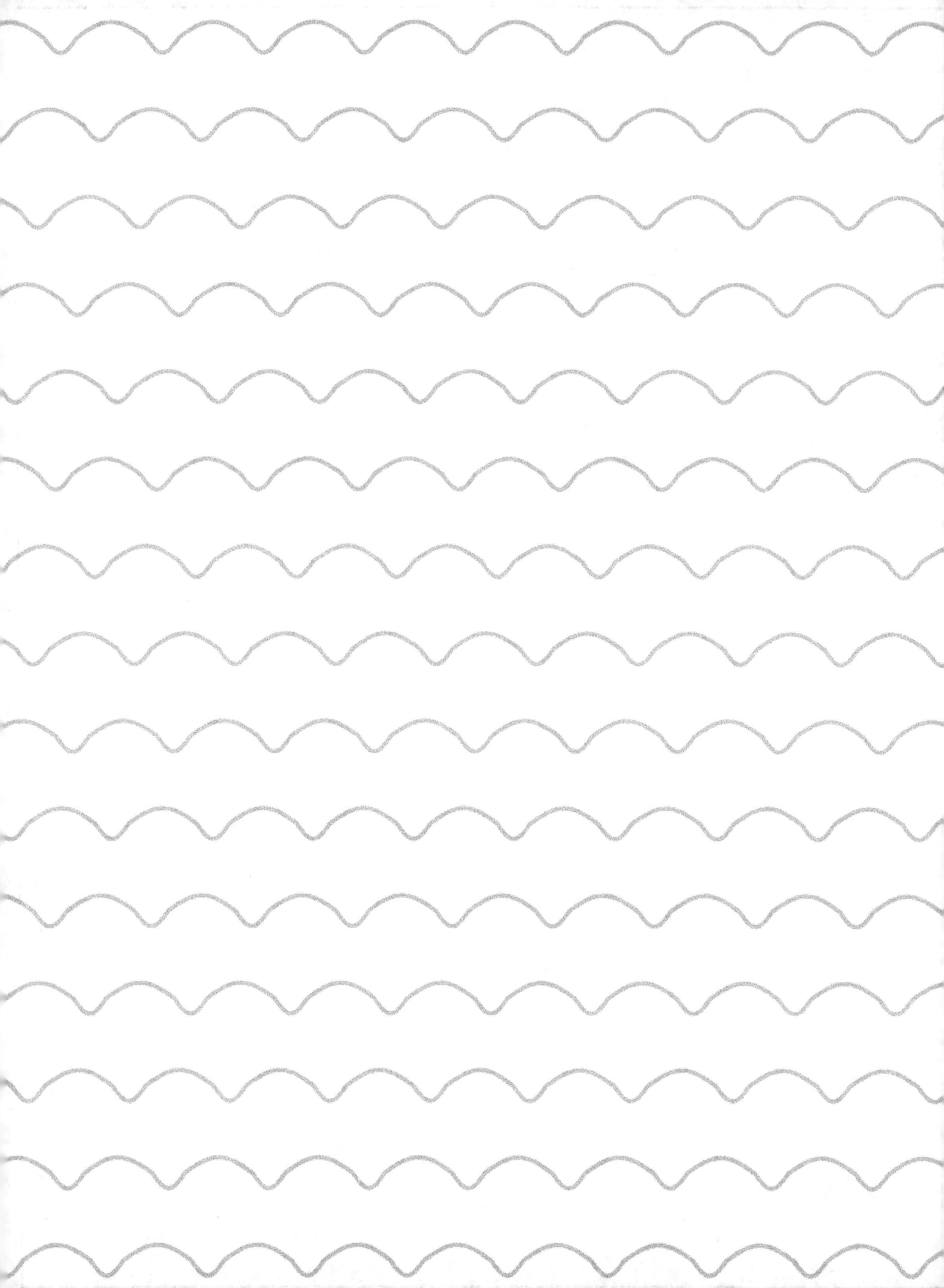

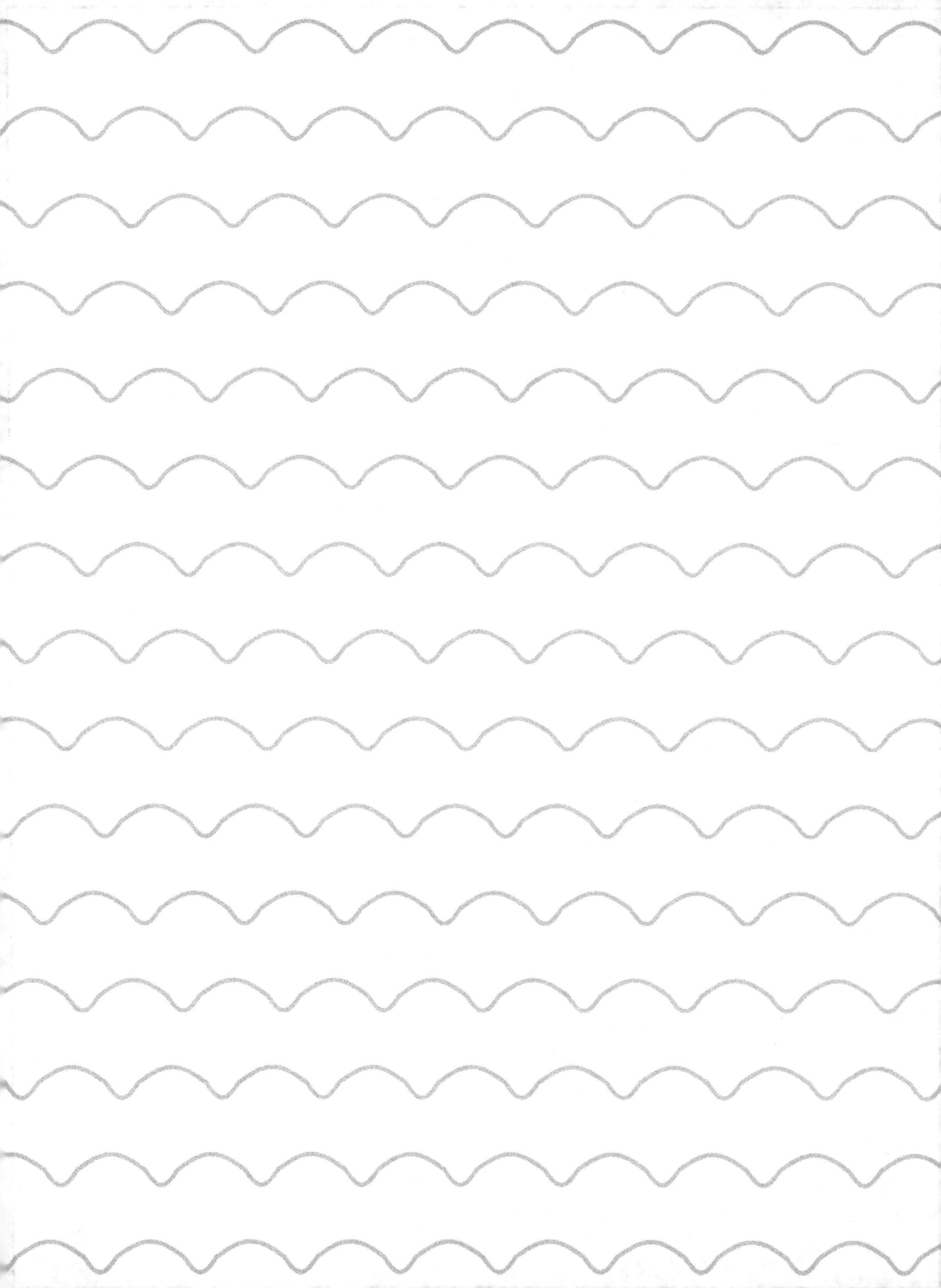

THANKS FOR COLORING!

Be Sure To Look
For Other
Adult Coloring Books
In The
'Color With Crayons'
Series On Amazon!

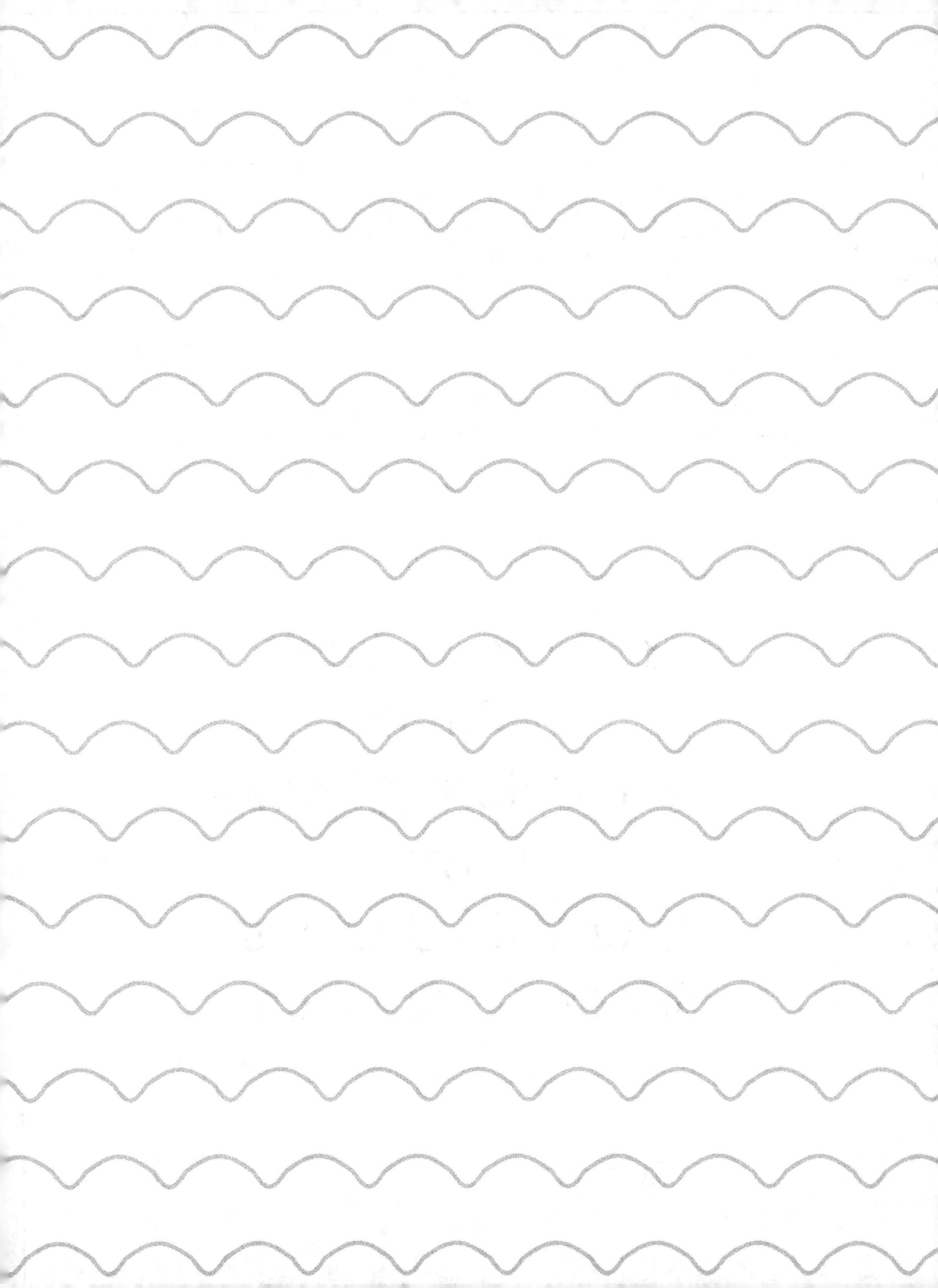